The Swing Back by Tridib Chaudhuri

ISBN-13: 978-1468104349

The Swing Back
Tridib Chaudhuri

CONTENTS

Prefatory

The present brochure seeks, in the main, to pass a critical review on the devious zig-zags in the fundamental political line of the Communist Party of India since 1947 from the standpoint of Marxism-Leninism (as distinguished from Stalinism), and to understand in that background the trend of the changes that have been taking place in CPI strategy and tactics from sometimes past consequent on the well-known Cominform directive of January 27. The Party does not seem to have completed the process of its assimilation of the said directive, at the moment of writing these prefatory remarks. Nor have all sections of the party, or at least its dominant factions, as yet been able to adjust themselves psychologically to its obvious political and tactical implications. Different sections of the CPI leadership are still far from having made up their minds finally and the decisions of to-day may not be the last words of the party in the process of the working out of the new line. A few words of explanation are, therefore, called for.

One of the main conclusions that I have sought to draw from my examination of the international policy-line of Stalinism, and the foreign-policy manoeuvres of the USSR, round which all changes in the tactical line of the CPI (as well as that of every other Stalinist Communist Party in the world) invariably revolve, has been that the CPI will be compelled, step by step, to go back to a policy of open alliance and class-collaboration with the Indian bourgeoisie—at least with those sections of the bourgeoisie who may for the present be outside the ruling circles. Even the possibility of a return to the pre 1948 policy of all-out support to the Nehru Government as in the days of P.C. Joshi's leadership, and an united-front with the ruling Congress bourgeoisie also cannot, in my view, be totally ruled out. The latest developments

in connection with the Korean War, Pandit Nehru's

6

peace- proposals to Stalin and Truman and the official and non-official reactions of Communist leaders to these proposals reflecting a new friendliness to Nehru would go to confirm my conclusions in part at least.

From a critical analysis of the pointers contained in the Cominform Editorial article of January 27, and authoritative documents relating to the China-way which the CPI has been asked to follow I came to the further conclusion that any form of armed insurrectionary struggle directed against the Nehru Government would surely come to be disavowed in the present political context of India, by the dictates of practical expediency of the new policy of wooing the national bourgeoisie.

But the latest statement of Sardar Patel, Home-Minister in the Congress Government, seems to indicate that the 'national bourgeoisie' or its ruling circles at least, do not feel properly courted or wooed (the CPI might retort that they are not seeking to woo the aged Sardar at all, for they are not at all keen about hardened big-bourgeois representatives like Patel).

"Whatever shift may have taken place in the tactics of the Communist Party", told the Sardar the Indian Parliament the other day, "there has been absolutely no change in their fundamental strategy of seizing power through violent revolt." He has cited certain remarks by Dange and excerpts from official CPI documents, to prove his contention. Without entering into any discussion, about Sardar Patel's topsy-turvy notions about 'strategy' and 'tactics', it may safely be presumed that while the India Government has taken note of the shift in party's policy towards a sudden friendliness towards national bourgeoisie, middle classes, rich peasantry etc. on the plea of anti-imperialism, (only a change of 'tactics' in the Sardar' view) he was not at all satisfied and did not think that the CPI would really be inclined to abandon the armed form of struggle against his government altogether — at least in outlying rural areas where it has yet some nuisance- value from Patel's point of view. Mr. Jaiprakash Narain, the Socialist Party leader, is also chary of favourably considering the question of forming a united-front with the CPI, after the 'latest' reorientation of their policy on the same ground. Some sections in the dominant group in CPI leadership in the reconstituted Central Committee of the party also seem to be keen upon salvaging some part of the lingering romantic revolutionary miasma of the Ranadive period by seeking to suggest sometimes, that the China- way line of Cominform do actually involve the formation of liberation armies and fighting the Government of the imperialist- feudal-big bourgeois combine from outlying rural areas. Mr. Dange has however clearly stated, "We do not hold the view that in the present conditions armed insurrection is the only step to overthrow the Nehru Government and establish a People's Democratic State in India. That definitely is not on the agenda of the Party to-day" (*Cross Roads,* July 28, 1950). The CPI, CC has since announced that Mr. Dange's views were entirely his personal, and did not represent the Party's stand in all respects, but there are others besides Dange, who accept in toto the implications of Cominform directive, and agree with him that the Cominform directive definitely rules out tactics of armed action in any form in the present political context of India. The armed action, of which the Cominform directive spoke, refers in their opinion, to other Asian and South East Asian countries where proper conditions for such action had matured, but not in India. The decisive point in this respect is, however not what this or that stalinist leader feels but what the expediency-considerations of Soviet foreign-policy line with regard to India and the Nehru Patel Government, dictate.

What however I have been concerned to prove in this book, is not that the CPI, or the international Stalinist leadership, has actually gone over to a policy of all-out support to the Congress Government.

That certainly is neither my contention, nor would be a correct representation of the present-day Stalinist policy in India. But the swing-back from a policy of all-out opposition to the national bourgeoisie, and the conception of a People's

8

Democratic Revolution directed against the entire Indian capitalist class and the simultaneous building up of Socialism, to the old social- democratic Joshi-ite position of a united-front with the 'national' bourgeoisie (barring the top-notch section who stand for collaboration with Anglo-American imperialism) does certainly in my view open up the possibility, under certain circumstances, of the CPI coming out in the open in unconditional support of Nehru Government. In the present international context of a closer understanding between the Nehru Government and the Sino-Soviet bloc the likelihood of such a change in CPI policy should not seem so very improbable.

The apparent confusion that seems to reign over the leading sections of party today arises out of the dizziness of the swing. back from left to right, and the incidental competition amongst rival marionette leaders of Indian Stalinism jockeying for vantage position against each other.

In seeking to trace the international back-ground of the zigzags of CPI policy, the writer has been inevitably compelled to relate these to changes in Soviet foreign-policy manoeuvres. The reasons for this have been explained fully in the text itself. To avoid all misunderstanding it is necessary to briefly reiterate my attitude, and that of the party to which I have the honour to belong, to the whole question clearly, As Marxist-Leninists we believe that despite inevitable historical limitations imposed by conditions of an imperialist-capitalist encirclement, the Soviet Union represents the revolutionary Socialist traditions of October 1917. It has preserved, within the frame-work of its basic Socialist property relations, in the continually rising standard of living secured for the masses through a system of planned economy, and its remarkably successful achievements in the concrete work of Socialist construction, those higher Socialist and human values which October Revolution won for all progressive mankind.

It is the sacred task of all Marxist-Leninists and toiling

peoples all over the world, to rally to the defence of Soviet Union against all forms of external capitalist intervention and internal counter revolutionary attacks.

In the face of the gathering offensive of the imperialist-capitalist world against Soviet Union, the sympathy and solidarity of all Revolutionary Socialists, and the toiling masses, must be unhesitatingly and unconditionally mobilised on the side of Soviet Union against Anglo-American imperialism. The same attitude to a certain extent holds good mutahis mutandis with regard to the People's Republic of China (not a Socialist but a democratic Social-Reformist country though) vis-á-vis Anglo-America.

Defence of the Socialist Soviet Union cannot in the Marxist- Leninist view, be however interpreted as blind toeing of the diplomatic line of the Soviet State at any particular moment vis- a-vis imperialist-capitalist states surrounding it, and determining the fundamental line of strategy and tactics in any country, vis-á- vis the capitalist ruling classes in mimic pursuance of that line. We believe that international revolution against the forces of imperialism-capitalism-the marshalling and mobilising of the forces of revolution in different countries taking into full account the concrete realities of class-correlationship of forces in each country—is the best defence of the Soviet Union and the Soviet peoples.

By making theories of "Socialism and Communism in a single country" and "the collaboration and peaceful co-existence of Socialism and capitalism side by side" the fulcrum of their world policy, the present leaders of CPSU have however transformed the Leninist conception of defence of Soviet Union into an instrument of Soviet power politics vis-á-vis Anglo-America, totally divorced from the perspective of international Socialist Revolution. The meaning of the latest changes in the CPI line could be properly appreciated only in this context.

August 10, 1950
Tridib Chaudhuri

Right About Turn!

Cominform Fiat; January, 1950

Under directives from the Cominform the ever-changing political line of the Communist Party of India is Changing again! In 1947 it was a shift from 'right' to 'left'; this time it is to be a shift back from 'left' to right! -Not to the wrong sort of 'right', 'right reformism', which P.C. Joshi represented. It is to be the right sort of 'right', 'right-revolutionism' perhaps (or a left-reformism?), which is now being eagerly searched for, through the usual process of 'critical, self-critical' analysis in the light of the new revelation handed out from Cominform centre.

Ranadive Thesis; 1948

A little more than two years back at the time of the Second Congress of the CPI in Calcutta (February-March, 1948) the new leadership of the party under B.T. Ranadive proclaimed to a staggered rank and life, and to the political public at large, that for the past five years or more the party had been actually following a fundamentally mistaken line of policy-a right-reformist class- collaborationist policy at that-under the leadership of P.C. Joshi, the acclaimed CPI-boss of the 'People's War' period!

The 'People's War' was however over more than two years then. With the end of the war the correlationship between the world of Socialism and the world of Capitalism, between Soviet Union.and Anglo-American imperialism i.e., had changed altogether, asserted the new Political Thesis which was presented to the Congress by Ranadive. The balance was said to have shifted in favour of the world of Socialism against that of capitalism. 'People's Democracy' had come into existence in a number of Right About Turn!

Cominform Fiat; January, 1950

Under directives from the Cominform the ever-changing political line of the Communist Party of India is Changing again! In 1947 it was a shift from 'right' to 'left'; this time it is to be a shift back from 'left' to right! -Not to the wrong sort of 'right', 'right reformism', which P.C. Joshi represented. It is to be the right sort of 'right', 'right-revolutionism' perhaps (or a left-reformism?), which is now being eagerly searched for, through the usual process of 'critical, self-critical' analysis in the light of the new revelation handed out from Cominform centre.

Ranadive Thesis; 1948

A little more than two years back at the time of the Second Congress of the CPI in Calcutta (February-March, 1948) the new leadership of the party under B.T. Ranadive proclaimed to a staggerred rank and life, and to the political public at large, that for the past five years or more the party had been actually following a fundamentally mistaken line of policy-a right-reformist class- collaborationist policy at that- under the leadership of P.C. Joshi, the acclaimed CPI-boss of the 'People's War' period!

The 'People's War' was however over more than two years then. With the end of the war the correlationship between the world of Socialism and the world of Capitalism, between Soviet Union.and Anglo-American imperialism i.e., had changed altogether, asserted the new Political Thesis which was presented to the Congress by Ranadive. The balance was said to have shifted in favour of the world of Socialism against that of capitalism. 'People's Democracy' had come into existence in a number of East European countries as a "new state form of the rule of toiling People" and as an "intermediate transition stage" to Socialism.

The two Camps USSR Vs. Anglo-America

The world now stood divided-it was further asserted with some emphasis-into two camps. viz the anti-imperialist democratic camp led by the Soviet Union, and ranged against it there was the imperialist anti-democratic camp led by Anglo-America.

This changed correlationship of forces and the division of the World into two opposite camps expressed itself, according to the new Thesis, in the frantic efforts that Anglo-American imperialists were making to save the capitalist social order from its impending doom. It also expressed itself in the desperate offensive which Anglo-American imperialism had launched to rally together all reactionary forces in every country, including India, to prepare the ground for a new world war for the destruction of the Soviet Union and the People's Democracies.

Echo of Zhdanov Thesis

It will be apparent to the informed reader, that these formulations of the Ranadive Thesis about the changed correlationship of forces on the international plane, and the new alignment of powers, were but a literal word to word echo of the analysis of the post-war international situation which was put forward by the late A. Zhdanov, as the spokesman of the Soviet Communist Party [Zhdanov was one of the three Secretaries of the CPSU (B) under lvi. Stalin, who is the General Secretary], in course of his speech to the inaugural Cominform Conference held in Poland, in September, 1947'-('The International Situation'- by A. Zhdanov, Chaps. I & 11; Foreign Language Publishing House, Moscow).

The policy of People's War alliance with Anglo-American imperialism and the so-called bourgeois democracies (as well as with 'anti-fascist' bourgeois political parties) forged in the background of Anglo-US-Soviet collaboration against Nazi Germany and Japan continued unchanged for Stalinist

13

Communist parties in every country (not for Joshi alone in India!) during the first one year and a half after the close of the war, from September 1945 up to the meeting of the Council of Foreign Ministers (US Great Britain, France and the SU) in Moscow, in March and April 1947. It was hoped that the Anglo-American ruling circles could still be pursuaded, or forced by the organised pressure of democratic public opinion in their countries, to respect the terms of Yalta, Teheran and Potsdam Agreements with Soviet Union about post-war division of spoils, and co-operate with the latter in building up the basis of "enduring peace and a democratic post war settlement acceptable" to all concerned. It however became clear to the Soviet leaders gradually that with defeat of German and Japan, the common danger that had so long kept Anglo- American powers united in their uneasy alliance with USSR was gone, and that the imperialist ruling circles of USA and Great Britain had finally abandoned the old course of unity and close political and military co-operation with the Soviets. They were now passing over to a new policy-the policy of securing unchallenged world domination, an imperialist expansion for themselves, a policy which necessarily involved their coming into hostile clashes with the growing influence of the Soviet Union in Asia and Europe.

The war-time political and military collaboration with Anglo American imperialism, on which the whole ideological edifice of People's War alliance stood, was necessarily scrapped under the impact of post-war international developments.

People's War Alliance Scrapped

By the close of 1947 Communist parties outside Soviet Union were accordingly switched to a policy of all round resistance to Anglo-American imperialist plans and their aggressive intentions against the Soviet Union. The old line of international policy viz: that of strengthening the unity and alliance of the three powers on the basis of a common struggle against Fascism and for the defence of 'democracy', was no longer suited to that of the post-war world situation.

All Stalinist parties outside the Soviet Union, and more particularly the nine European Communist Parties which were associated in the Cominform, were directed to try their utmost to organise and throw up popular mass resistance under their leadership to the Anglo-American plans of imperialist expansion "along every line Government, economic and ideological."

Behind Ranadive's Enlightenment

The Ranadive formulation about "a fundamental shift" in the international correlationship of forces in the post-war period was derived from the above analysis; and was, as a matter of fact, nothing very original in itself. Neither Ranadive himself, nor any one of his supporters who came to the forefront in the Calcutta Congress of the CPI or thereafter, did come by their new found enlightenment, before the inaugural Cominform conference in September 1947, or the above referred Speech of A Zhdanov in that conference. None of the spokesmen of the new line of the CPI and upholders of the new thesis did feel any urge in themselves to raise the question of a change of the fundamental line of policy of the party in the light of altered international situation of the post-war period any time before December 1947, i.e., three months after the trend of discussion and decisions of the Cominform conference became known. The post-war period was already more than two years old. But nobody yet felt the necessity of taking note of what was but a very obvious and long anticipated development in the international situation viz: the inevitable break- up of Anglo-US-Soviet alliance in absence of the common cause, once Germany and Japan were defeated. An acquaintance with the elements of Marxism-Leninism, or even plain commonsense, should have aroused anticipation of this inevitable development which was bound to result from the basic contradiction between

15

Soviet Socialism and Anglo-American imperialism.

The cue was handed : International situation changes at last!

But nothing changes in the Stalinist pattern of thought, without the cue of that change coming from the highest directive centre of their world-thought viz: the leadership of the CPSIJ itself. The cue was eventually handed in September 1947 in the shape of the new Zhdanov formulation about the altered post-war international situation. The international situation became changed almost overnight for all Stalinist Communist parties. The majority of the old Central Committee of the CPI, for instance, refused in June, 1947 to regard the Mountbatten Plan for the division of India and transfer of power to the Congress and the Muslim League as a deal between British imperialism and the Indian bourgeoise as their mutual safeguard against the rising revolutionary upsurge of the toiling masses. They preferred to look at it more as "an important concession" which the relatively progressive Labour Government of Britain (Labour victory in British election was regarded as 'a victory of popular forces' till then!) was forced to make "to the urgent demands of the national liberation movement of the Indian people" against the stiff resistance of imperialist vested-interests as a result of popular democratic mass pressure both in British -and in this country. At home the British labour movement "would not back the reconquest of India." All over the world, democratic opinion "immensely strengthened by the victory over Fascism," demanded Indian independence to which British imperialism was now compelled perforce to bow down. Their reading of the international and national situations in terms of the then current official Stalinist categories of thought thus led them to see even in the diabolical Mountbatten Plan an indirect "victory of the popular forces." In December 1947, however, after the new Zhdanov formulation became known in this country, the majority of the same old Central Committee suddenly woke to the fact that the international situation had after all "undergone a fundamental change" in the post-war period, which called for a change in the formulation of the fundamental line of policy of the party in India also, a change in the characterisation of the Mountbatten Plan, as well as that of the relationship of the Nehru Government and the Indian bourgeoisie with Anglo-American imperialism. The Mountbatten Award was from now on to be seen not as "a retreat of imperialism", "but as a cunning counter-offensive against the rising forces of the Indian people", a plan for "the subservient collaboration of Indian capitalists and landlords with British imperialism." (see CPI CC statement on Mountbatten Award and the December 1947 Policy Statement.)

The New Qualitative Change: Imperialism escapes From 'The Camp Of People'

It was almost like the sudden 'qualitative change' in the character of the imperialist war in 1941 after Nazi attack on Soviet Union and the forging of the Anglo-Soviet-US alliance against Nazi Germany; the direction of the change this time however being in the opposite direction. In 1941 Anglo-American imperialism had become "prisoners in the camp of the people" and were forced to collaborate with the Soviet Union against Nazi Germany in order to save themselves. In 1947-48 these two imperialist powers must have some-how again managed to escape from "the people's camp." They were now desperately trying to overthrow and destroy that camp and actually preparing to unleash a new war of aggression against the Soviet Union. The international situation must, therefore, have changed necessarily, specially when the fact of the change was now duly noted by Soviet Communist leadership officially. The latter had also laid down the new line of policy that was to be followed by all fraternal CP-s in the background of this change, through the Cominform. There was, therefore, no longer any scope for unnecessary theoretical vacillations.

17

Discovery Of Bourgeois Line-up With Imperialism

In every country, including India, the bourgeoisie and their servitors were now seen clearly lining up with Anglo-American imperialism. In India this line-up might have been doubtful when the Mountbatten Plan was actually announced and accepted by the Congress in June 1947. But in December 1947, or February- March 1948, when the Congress Government was working under the very same Mountbatten Plan which they had accepted in June 1947, it could no longer be held in doubt. It came to be announced with a certain amount of flourish, as if a very wonderful discovery was made, that by accepting the Mountbatten Plan the Nehru Government in India had openly joined hands with Anglo- American imperialism. There could, therefore, be no longer any talk of a difference between the confirmed right-winger Patel or the so-called "progressive" Nehru as the old Joshi-ite Central Committee thought. The entire Indian bourgeoisie as a whole, as represented by the leadership of the Indian National Congress and the Congress Government under Nehru and Patel, had really after all, gone over to imperialism.

The Congress Government had to be opposed therefore by all means at the disposal of the CPI. The foreign policy of the Nehru Government was actually nothing but a policy of collaboration with Anglo-American imperialism. Under cover of 'neutrality' and 'third bloc' it only sought to keep India away from the democratic camp (the Soviet camp i.e.) and had opened the way to India's line-up with the imperialist camp.

CPI Breaks with Joshi's 'Reformism'

Joshi's policy of all-out support to Nehru and the Congress 'national' Government was under these circumstances nothing but a piece of unalloyed "opportunist right-reformism," according to Ranadive and his supporters. It was the inevitable result of Joshi's clear deviations from the true Leninist path of revolutionary Marxism. The Joshi line was simply a case in

18

instance of "reformist petty-bourgeois revisionism masquerading under the garb of Marxism." The Communist Party and its rank and file were called upon by Ranadive to finally break with the reformism of Joshi-ite leadership which prevailed in the party for the past five years or more.

The Second Congress of the Communist Party was supposed to have done this, i.e. *decisively* broken with past reformist mistakes and class collaborationism of Joshi once for all.

It was hailed in CP Press all over India, as well as outside India, as marking "a great turning point in the history" of the party and a supreme example of "a magnificent united initiative of the rank-and-file delegates and the leadership of the Party in evolving a revolutionary line, policy and tactics in a period of revolutionary crisis in India" (Review of the Second Congress of the Communist Party of India P. 29).

"As a result of this Congress"-it was claimed, "the party emerges solidly united behind the new revolutionary line and behind the new leadership, ready to go into action with firm faith in Marxism-Leninism, and full confidence in the revolutionary spirit of the masses ...lt *did honour* to the rank and file delegates and leadership of the party, to their loyalty to the principles of Marxism and Leninism' (ibid).

Enter Ranadive! Exit Joshi!

This was in February-March 1948. Joshi was dropped from General Secretaryship and from the Central Committee of the party as well. A new Central Committee with B. T. Ranadive the pet 'left' doctrinaire of the party, and supposed to be the most determined fighter against all shades of overt or covert reformist deviations-was elected to lead the party on the newly discovered revolutionary line. The Central Committee elected in this Congress contained,The official report of the Party Congress said, a majority of those members who had fought for this new line, as *the only correct one for the party* to adopt in

19

the changed national and international situation.

The communist rank-and-file, who were hitherto taught to regard the CPI line always correct, whatever might be the temporary turns and twists of its strategy and tactics, received a rather severe mental jolt to learn that they had been following a fundamentally incorrect and thoroughly reformist line of policy all these years under boss Joshi's leadership, whom they were made to look upon more as an infallible demigod than an ordinary mortal. Some remembered with pangs the episode of the spirited protest of Soli Batliwala against Joshi's line of collaboration with imperialism and his expulsion by the old Polit-Bureau and Central Committee in which, curiously enough Comrade B. T. Ranadive was also a member. Why did he not raise his voice against Batliwala's expulsion then?

In spite of these disturbing notes of interrogation in their minds they were eventually persuaded to re-inforce themselves in their wonted confidence in the wisdom of the party with the re- assuring thought, that whatever might have been the mistakes of the party in the past under the reformist leadership of Joshi, it had now found the "correct" line after all, an orthodox "revolutionary" line, true to the basic teachings of Marxism-Leninism.

The 'new' revolutionary line

It was no longer a line, moreover, of shameless collaboration with the war efforts of hated Anglo-American imperialism foisted on the party by the arch-reformist Joshi during the 'People's War' days, which had brought any amount of shame and popular odium upon the very name 'Communist'. Nor was it a 'line of grovelling obsequiously' before Gandhi, Nehru and the reformist bourgeoisie, or lending indirect support to the communal demands of the Muslim League in the name of *national* self-determination. This time it was to be a consistently militant and revolutionary political line, a proletarian class line of total opposition to the collaborationist bourgeoisie and the

Congress Government under whose oppression the masses were groaning literally. The masses were becoming increasingly disillusioned with the Congress Government and any opposition to it was bound to be popular. The Communist Party might of course, have committed very serious mistakes in the past. Which party does not? But only a genuinely Bolshevik, Stalinist Communist Party like the CPI knows how to correct these mistakes in a 'revolutionary' way, in the light of Marxism-Leninism; and again throw up an adequate revolutionary leadership, fitted in every way to guide the party in the new 'correct' line.

Outside Communist ranks, the new political line of the CPI, as formulated by the 1948 Calcutta Thesis under Ranadive's leadership came to be regarded in certain 'leftist' circles also, as a welcome change from past reformist betrayals of the People's War period. It entitled the CPI, in their eyes, to re-entry into the ranks of revolutionary anti-imperialist fighters, and the confidence of the masses. It was therefore held up by the new leaders of the party as a sort of an 'achievement' of which the party could be legitimately proud of, and on which it could claim the congratulation of all genuine leftists and Marxist-Leninists in the country.

'Left' turn in international Stalinism

In common with Stalinist Communist parties all over the world the entire Indian Communist Party was thus switched to the 'left' in 1948. The Cominform had already been brought into existence some months before (September 1947). A clearly discernible 'left' orientation in international Stalinist strategy and tactics was initiated under he forceful leadership of late Andrei Zhdanov. Communist Parties everywhere were asked to engage in "the historic task of leading and organising resistance to the Anglo-American imperialist war-mongers all along the line." The long-drawn negotiations of the Chinese CP for a coalition with Chiang Kai-shek were also finally broken off and the party took to the path of armed resistance and Civil War against American- backed KMT. The Communist Parties in Eastern Europe also threw overboard about this time, the policy of uneasy coalition with bourgeois parties maintaining sympathetic political contacts with Anglo-America, and began to push themselves to a position of unchallenged supremacy in the governments of their countries, with the assurance of Soviet military and political backing guaranteed before hand. Even British, French and Italian CP-s were induced to take up a pronouncedly fighting and militant tone and tried to organise large-scale political strikes and other political demonstrations. The CP. USA unceremoniously dropped Earl Browder from leadership and reorganised itself under the avowed 'leftist' William Foster. The shift to the 'left' which occurred in the political line of policy of the CPI about this time therefore came to be justified as following from the new 'left' orientation of the international movement and to have the tacit approval of international leadership. It was hailed with approval in Stalinist press abroad as "a great step." Thus the new party-line naturally came to be regarded by the CPI rank-and-file as the only "correct" line consistent with the new left orientation of the international movement. No opposition to the new line was therefore voiced in the Congress. Everybody there was only too eager to prove himself completely outgrown from the past reformist mistakes. Even P. C. Joshi himself was stampeded into admitting his past errors and had to promise unconditional support to the new line of policy adopted by the Second Congress.[1]

Notes

1. That however did not prevent his suspension and subsequent expulsion from the party like Browder in USA

Since Calcutta Thesis

"Pure" Marxism of Ranadive

The Political thesis adopted at the Second Congress, provided, it should be noted, the starting point only. In course of the next two years new 'reformist mistakes' and new 'deviations' were successively netted up and condemned. The party line seemed to grow ever more immaculate, flawless and 'purely' Marxist day by day, through a process of ideo-chemical distillation and purging. All hidden reformist vestiges of the Joshi-period were mercilessly exposed and hunted out. Armed with a 'correct' revolutionary strategy and tactics the party now seemed to have earned the right to the confidence of all sections of the toiling people and the working classes. It could now easily hope to lead the masses to direct action and unleash a mighty revolutionary mass onslaught against the bourgeoisie and the Congress Government.

New 'revolutionary' upsurge

A new revolutionary mass upsurge—a veritable People's Democratic Revolution—was thus envisaged throwing itself up, just round the corner. It only remained for the party to come forward and take up the leadership of that 'revolution.' The elemental force of postwar mass-upsurge as evidenced by the INA movement, naval mutiny & worker's strikes, the 'Tebhaga' movement etc, had by no means diminished or become exhausted. The masses were thoroughly disillusioned. "Never was there", it was asserted in the Calcutta Thesis, "so much understanding of the main slogans of the democratic movement." Out of the disillusionment of the masses the demand for an alternative Government was bound to arise soon; and it was the duty of the Communist Party to consciously guide the people in fighting for that demand boldly and decisively. The call was therefore given for the formation of a "Democratic Front" based on the alliance of the workers, peasants and the oppressed petty-bourgeoisie under the leadership of the working class and the communist Party. This "Democratic Front" was to form the basis of the new state-power of the toiling people and the new government after the overthrow of the present bureaucratic system.

Call to 'action' Armed Resistance

Decked with properly couched official People's Democratic terminology of international Stalinism, a call was thus given in effect for the immediate launching of revolutionary mass struggles against the Congress Governments all over the country. Under the impact of the crisis and as the result of growing disillusionment amongst the masses with the Congress Government "larger and larger sections of masses will be set in motion" it was confidently hoped. The party rank and file were, therefore, straight away ordered to throw "themselves at the head of this imaginary mass upsurge. We need hardly enter into the detailed history of these "revolutionary" mass-actions under the leadership of the Communist Party and their outcomes. Working class and peasant detachments in isolated areas, widely separated from each other, were thrown into the firing line to face rifle and machine-gun bullets of the armed forces of the Government.

'The Telengana Way'

The armed rising of the peasants in the Telengana area of Hyderabad against feudal Jagirdars there, were held up as a sort of fore-runner of the coming all-national uprising. The peculiar correlationship of forces in the unsettled conditions of Hyderabad after 'transfer of power' and the withdrawal of British Government from the formal position of suzerainty over the Native States, were not taken into account. The tussle between the feudal Nizam Government and the Central Government of the Indian Union under the national bourgeois leadership of the Congress, the democratic struggle of the

Hyderabad people against the absolutism of Nizam, the struggle of the Communal Fascist Razakars both against the democratic, State-people's movement and against any encroachment of the Nizam's dominions by the Indian Union, and the simultaneous anti-Deshmukh (as the big feudal lords were called in this area) struggle of the Telengana peasants—all these going on simultaneously, often merging, often cutting across each other, created a general confusion which enabled the peasant revolt in the outlying Telengana area to take on an armed character with comparative ease than might be possible elsewhere. But without any reference to the specific features of the Telengana movement and to the feasibility of creating favourable conditions for armed insurrection elsewhere in the country outside Telengana, the entire party was called upon by the Party leadership to go the "Telengana way."

Ranks to the Firing Line

The disastrous consequences of this adventurist policy can be easily imagined. The full brunt of the repressive onslaughts of Congress capitalist reaction inevitably came down on the heads of the masses. In the absence of any prior preparation, neither the organisation nor the resources of the party could give them any protection. In most cases. they were left to their own devices to withstand the terrible fury of barbaric police and military repression. "Because it was a revolutionary period" a subsequent document of the CPI leadership argued in justification of this adventurism, "the most elementary forms of struggle will set in motion forces which will enable the masses to overcome" their present "backwardness "and the "limited perspectives" of their consciousness. Honest rank-and-filers idealistically inspired, were peremptorily ordered to throw themselves at the head of the masses, try to give the character of armed seizure-of-power struggle to every sporadic mass-action they happened to lead, face bullets, and if necessary to court death—which they often did at the bidding of the leaders—imagine all the time that they were perhaps carrying out the behests of a correct, "revolutionary" Marxist-Leninist line, and taking the red flag of proletarian revolution and people's democracy one step further forward.

Leaders engaged in distillation of 'pure' Marxism

The leaders were of course, either secure behind prison bars or U.G. (underground). They were supposed to be engaged all the time in higher 'ideological' struggles for ridding the party of all doubters and vacillators, suspending this comrade, repremanding that, expelling some other. Entire Provincial Committees, were suspended, dissolved and reconstituted. The party line was thus being continually distilled ever more sublime and becoming flawlessly "correct" everyday, in true Marxist- Leninist-Stalinist fashion. Both leadership and rank and file were serenely happy at that reassuring thought.

Chorus of Balabusheviches!

It was on in this way for two years uninterruptedly without the Cominform and the international Stalinist leadership feeling the slightest necessity of making any intervention in the affairs of, the Communist Party of India. The noted Soviet specialist on India A. M. Dyakov mentioned with approval the programme of the Second Congress of the CPI in his book "New Stage in India's Liberation Struggle" which was published shortly after the Calcutta Congress. The Calcutta Thesis and the Report of the Second Congress were reproduced in Stalinist organs abroad in quite eulogistic terms. Not only that, even as late as the last quarter of 1949, the CPI was being complimented by the Soviet Specialists in highly appreciative tones. The national liberation movement of India had entered "a new stage" after the war, wrote V. Balabushevich in the pages of the Soviet Journal *'Problems of Economics'* (No. 8) under the leadership of the working class and the Communist Party. The Second Congress of the Communist Party of India was characterised as before as "an important step" in the life of the party, and a big political event inside the country." The programme of the Second Congress had in short the unstinted approval of Balabushevich.

He seemed quite confident that the influence of, the communist Party had "increased considerably" both in India and Pakistan—thanks to the "correct revolutionary formulation" of its tasks in that programme which "expresses the aspirations and hopes of the broadest masses of the Indian people." Whether amongst the peasantry or the urban petty-bourgeoisie and students, Balabushevich saw nothing and heard nothing, except the steadily growing "influence of the working class and the Communist Party." The Telengana struggle was also hailed by him as "the first attempt at creating People's Democracy in India" and the "harbinger of the coming agrarian revolution." With reference to the petty-bourgeoisie and the students—their active participation in the *"mass militant political actions* taking place under the leadership of the Communist Party"—was mentioned in terms of highest approbation. Every where there was nothing but "a steady growth" of the influence and the prestige of the Communist Party and its leadership. ('New stage in the National Liberation Struggle' in India—*Problems of Economics;* No. 8)

Quandary of the Rank-and-filers

Politically conscious people in India and the masses themselves of course knew better. Even large sections of CPI adherents would have a different story to tell here on spot, than that recounted by Balabushevich from distant Soviet Union. But in general upto to the end of 1949, neither the Cominform nor the leading theoreticians of the CPSU and world-Stalinism for the matter of that, afforded any reason for the ordinary rank-and-file workers of the CPI to think that their Party leadership was moving in a wrong way, or that the political line of the party as set by the Second Congress deviated from the path of

27

true Marxist-Leninist rectitude in any way.

Soviet interests 'served aright'

Balabushevich and others of his ilk could however afford to be complacent. The CPI organised a peace-rally at Firozabad in UP and had a resolution passed to the effect that "under no circumstances will the Indian workers ever take up arms against the Soviet Union" and expressed their "determination to give full rebuff to imperialist attempts to convert India into a war-base for an attack against the Soviet Union." Balabusheviches were satisfied; their interests seemed served aright for the present by their henchmen in India. They were hardly concerned with anything else much less with objective realities confronting the working class movement in this country.

Cominformation from the blue!

On the 27th of January, 1950 the Cominform organ *"For a Lasting peace; For a People's Democracy"*however unexpectedly came out with an editorial article on the national liberation movements in colonial and dependent countries, which contained a new and a fundamentally different formulation of the tasks before the Communists in India. This article completely cut the ground from beneath the political formulation of the Second Congress of the CPI adopted two years back and all its subsequent elaborations. The article contained no adverse criticism against the Calcutta Thesis of the Communist Party as such. But its fundamental political and theoretical implications were unmistakably clear. If one were to accept the line of the Cominform Editorial as correct, the Calcutta thesis and all political formulations made by the CPI leadership from time to time for the guidance of party-cadres during these two years, automatically stood condemned and could not but be regarded as being based on fundamentally mistaken notions. There was absolutely no getting away from this unpleasant fact.

The line of the Calcutta Thesis was supposed, to have 'set right' the reformist mistakes and betrayals of the past five years and more. In 1948 the Second Congress line seemed to have been the only 'correct' line. But two years later the party was called upon all of a sudden to throw overboard and repudiate this 'correct' revolutionary line, which was one time supposed to have rather "done honour" to the party leadership and the rank and file, a line which in the words of Batabushevich "expressed the aspirations and hopes of the broadest masses of the Indian people" and had contributed so much to "the steady growth of the influence of the party amongst the masses"—as fundamentally mistaken, misconceived and even anti-Marxist!

Tragi-Comedy of Errors!

At the altar of Leaders' mistakes!

Was the history of the Communist Party to be looked upon then as nothing but a string of ideological and political errors, a succession of petty-bourgeois opportunist deviations and anti Marxist betrayals of the working-class cause? Logically such a conclusion seems almost irresistible? And, what about those heroic rank-and-file fighters who were ordered to the firing line and fell fighting, facing machine-gun bullets and rifle volleys unflinchingly in the conviction that they were sacrificing their lives for carrying out the correct revolutionary line of the party, in order to prepare the grounds for a People's Democratic Revolution and the rule of toilers? It now seems that they were as a matter of fact following a "petty-bourgeois" "opportunist" line, and were sacrificed only to satisfy the whims of certain wrongheaded leaders. Besides, what about the scores of militant working class and peasant cadres who had to take upon themselves the terrible fury of police and military onslaughts and were literally massacred at the altar of the mistaken lines of policy of the politically imbecile leadership of a party which only knows how to replace one mistake by another?

Questions left unanswered

Who were to pay for these lives and recompense their sacrifice? Why could not the international leadership intervene earlier? Why it went on irresponsibly shouting approval at every step taken by CPI, Balabushevich fashion, and encouraging the utterly irresponsible CPI leadership to persist doggedly in justifying their terrific mistakes and the wanton waste of human lives and resources at the disposal of the party? Why now, when all this mischief is done and eyes kept deliberately shut all the time, is the rank-and-file worker being asked to repudiate unceremoniously the very same leadership who had "earned the gratitude of the entire working class", were they told to rescue the Communist Party from the rut of Joshi-ite right-reformism and class-collaboration with a "new revolutionary" Marxist-Leninist formulation of the task before the party and by their programme of the "Democratic Front"? There was no proper explanation.

A New 'shift'?

The allegedly right-reformist Joshi-ite leadership was repudiated in the name of a fundamental 'shift' in the international correlationship of forces between the Soviet Union and Anglo- America after the war, of a new alignment of classes both on the national and the international plane which joshi failed to evaluate properly or to take note of. But what is the 'new' shift in international situation which makes the repudiation and denunciation of the Ranadive line historically imperative now?

No satisfactory answer has been vouched by international Stalinism on this score either, uptil now, at least directly.

No answer again

Stalinist theoreticians in this country-some of them enthusiastic supporters of Ranadive till the other day-seem to think that it is not a question of any new 'shift' in the international alignment of forces having occurred in the meantime. It is more a question of fundamentally misunderstanding the significance of the changes that had taken place in the post-war period, of over- estimating certain aspects and under-estimating others, of running too far ahead of the actual historical possibilities of the situation and a bit too fast. Ranadive, according to his defenders, took into account the post-war division of world forces and the new international situation all right. But he had misunderstood the actual significance of this division and the political consequences to which- it was leading. But if that be really so, why he was not pulled up by the international Stalinist leadership[1], or by our national stalinists either, these two years? Or has the Ranadive line, which was relatively correct in 1948, suddenly become incorrect now it 1950, owing to some mysterious 'qualitative' change in the national or international situation? There again, we have no clear cut answer.

The 'True' Bolshevik Lenin-Stalin Line!

The only fact that stands out above everything else is the formulation of anew line of political strategy and tactics for Indian Communists by the Cominform and discarding of the line which held ground for the last two years.

From now onwards this will in its turn be the "new revolutionary line"and the "only correct" Lenin-Stalin line at that. Just as the Ranadive Thesis embodied the "only correct" Marxist-Leninist revolutionary line in February-March 1948, or in the period between 1948-50; just as the Joshi line was the "only correct" line of "concrete" Marxism in the National Front and People's War phases, so now we are again presented with another "correct line"-the author this time being the international Stalinist leadership of the Cominform, as represented by the LPPD- Editorial Board. Who will dare to say that it is not the "true" Marxist-Leninist formulation, till it is repudiated in its turn and replaced by a new formulation of political strategy equally "correct," equally "revolutionary" and having equal claim to "true" Marxist-Leninist-Stalinist wisdom? The CPI, so it seems has the wonderful knack of having been always in the right in the 'immediate present". It always follows the "correct", "scientific" Marxist-Leninist line, the "true" Bolshevik Lenin-Stalin line- with one qualification however, that is, it always does so "in the present." But subsequently it always discovers itself having strayed from the correct Marxist-Leninist path "in the past" and to have committed all sorts of "opportunist" mistakes, right- reformism, left-sectarianism,

33

Trotsky-ism, Titoism and all other crimes known in Stalinist vocabulary.

From People's War to People's Front

In 1936-37 Joshi, made wiser by his new-found enlightenment from the Dutt-Bradley thesis (the Programme which was then drafted for the CPI by Ben Bradley and R. P. Dutt of the Communist Party of Great Britain) found the past policy of the party since 1934 to have consisted of a series of ultra-left, sectarian and isolationist mistakes, which prevented the party from taking up its rightful place in the national mass-struggle against imperialism, as its builder, initiator and principal leader. In those days, he claimed to have found the "only correct" revolutionary path-the path of "United National Front" with reformist Congress bourgeoisie. The National front tactics of class- collaboration and unconditional support of the bourgeois-reformist Gandhi-Nehru leadership inside the Congress was then forced down the throats of the party as the only correct application of the Anti-Fascist Popular Front tactics formulated by Dimitrov in the Seventh World Congress of the Comintern. This anti-Fascist masquerade was however given up as soon as the Soviet Union entered into a Non-Agression Pact with Nazi Germany and the war started. So long as the war remained confined between the Nazi and Fascist powers on one side and Anglo-French imperialism on the other,-it was regarded as an imperialist war with Great Britain and France (and not Nazi Germany!) as the main aggressors. After the occupation of Western Poland by the Nazis, and the entry of the Soviet Army in Eastern Poland by aggreement with Nazi Germany, Britain and irance were indicated as "aggressive war-mongers who having taken the path of war do not want to leave it"-because they had rejected the Nazi proposals for peace on the basis of the recognition of Soviet- German occupation of Poland. It continued in this way for the first 21 months of the war.

From People's War to Post-War

With the attack against Soviet Union by Nazi Germany in June 1941, we all know how the character of the war became "qualitatively" changed for communists all over the world. In India the CP persisted, for the first few months, in opposing the war-efforts of British imperialism without taking into account this "qualitative" change in the character of the war from that of an imperialist war to an "Anti-Fascist People's War". In November- December 1941 the leadership obtained the new authoritiative version of the "correct" Marxist-Leninist-Stalinist line from CPGB by way of Ceylon, and came to realise that they had been pursuing a fundamentally mistaken line these six months, a line of "Jawharlalist"-nationalist deviation[2] from the "true" path of Lenin Stalin and internationalism!

This deviation was however corrected in time and the right royal People's War alliance with Anglo-American imperialism came into operation from November 1941.

The People's War line of collaboration with imperialism, and that with the reformist national bourgeoisie continued to be regarded as "unmistakably correct" as late as December 1947 i.e. for more than two years after the war. Between December 1947 and March 1948 however the party again came by new revolutionary enlightenment and discovered that the line of policy formulated by Joshi in 1941, and followed unhesitatingly by the party rank and file for a period of more than five years, was fundamentally incorrect and anti-Marxist. It constituted nothing but a string of right-reformist class-collaborationist deviations leading practically to a line of "abject surrender to the national bourgeoisie and a marked decrease in the sharpness of the Party's struggle against imperialism." It led the party to think in terms of a "peaceful development of independence and socialism and to abjure struggle" etc.

"Pure" Marxism of Ranadive also goes wrong!

Taking the cue from Zhadanov and the Cominform, the

party was however enabled to overcome these "gross reformist deviations" this time also, and forge another 'correct' Marxist line in 1947-48 under the leadership of Ranadive. Armed with this rediscovery of the "Correct" revolutionary line, it went into action with a firm faith in its "Marxism-Leninism" and "full of confidence" in the revolutionary spirit of the masses.

But even this revolutionary line now transpires in retrospect to have been a fundamentally anti-Marxist, anti-Lenin-Stalin, left sectarian opportunist line!

Notes:

1. Soon after the Second Congress of the CPI in Calcutta the 'Bolshevik', the theoretical organ of the Communist Party of the Soviet Union, contained an article by M. Alexyev in its issue of June 15, 1948 which reviewed the decisions of the Congress and may be said to have made alternative formulations on certain points e. g. on the role of the Indian bourgeoisie.It spoke of the Indian big bourgeoisie only as collaborating with Anglo- American imperialism. The Calcutta Thesis did not specially mention the 'big' bourgeoisie and gave an impression that it was up against the entire Indian bourgeoisie as collaborationist. Mr. P.C. Joshi, thinks that it ought to have been regarded as a warning to the new CPI leadership against their Ultra-leftism. But unfortunately the whole article of M. Alexyev was interpersed with such encomiums for the CPI and the Second Congress that it could hardly be regarded as such by any body without much hair-splitting interpretation of terms (Sec: "Views by P.C. Joshi" No. 1).

2. Because Pandit Jawaharlal Nehru wanted to oppose British imperialism and its war efforts in spite of his professed sympathy for the 'democratic' Anglo-US Soviet coalition against Nazi Germany & Japan. This was due to Jawaharlal's 'nationalist' weakness. The continued oppoisition ofthe CPI, during the first five months of the Soviet-German war, to SU's 'democratic' ally Britain was likewise put down to 'nationalist' deviations.

Self-Criticism?

Mistakes chasing each other!

It has continued in this way for the past sixteen years of the history of the CPI—of one series of mistakes replacing another and being replaced in turn by newer ones. Infantile left-communism of the initial adolescent years (1934-35) was 'corrected' by right-reformism and class-collaboration introduced on the pleas of United National Front and subsequently on that of an Anti-Fascist People's War (1936-47). This was 'corrected' in its turn by a new version of earlier Leftism—now discovered to be nothing other than 'left-opportunism' (1948-50). This is now sought to be put right by a more subtle form of class-collaboration on the plea of a fight for the defence of national independence and sovereignty, against Anglo-American imperialism and their big-bourgeois Indian collaborators for People's Democracy! This may pershaps be again found to have concealed some novel kind of mistake under convenient theoretical trappings. Or even this might prove "too left". Who knows? It will all depend on the kind of 'shift' that occurs in the international correlationship of forces. If past experience proves any guide for coming events, we are to be confronted for some time with another spate of 'self-critical' penance for the expiation of past sins, of 'critical, self-critical' heart-searchings, and confessions of all sorts of deviations from the true Lenin-Stalin path. There will be fresh declarations of "firm Bolshevik determination" for the undoing of past mistakes, of making a complete turn and working back to the "true" revolutionary path by mercilessly exposing and fighting these mistakes. We are already witnessing that inevitable process of self-critical confession of guilt by the CPI Polit-Boureau and its leading cadres of Provincial and District units by instalments every month these days.

Expiation by instalments!

The CPI Polit-Boureau itself was perhaps no less confused and bewildered this time than the rank-and-file, after the publication of Cominform Editorial. They could hardly believe that after all the buck-up that they received from Soviet publicists like Dyakov and Balabushevich they could be let down so suddenly and so soon without any warning, as was done by the Cominform Editorial of January 27. It took more than one month for CPI leadership and Mr. B.T. Ranadive to decide what to do. The Cominform article was not given any publicity in CPI-press for more than a month. Ranadive then came out with a short statement hailing the Editorial article in LPPD as "a great contribution to the understanding of the problems of national liberation struggle in India" and "fully accepted" its conclusions. It was also announced that the article could be "an invaluable weapon" in the hands of the Communist Party for removing all "errors and mistakes" that hampered its growth. This was the first indirect admission by the CPI leadership that any "mistakes and errors" were involved in the policy hitherto followed by them, which might have hampered the growth of the party. But there was no indication of the nature or significance of these mistakes.

'Only a little dogmatism'!

In the middle of March, the Polit-Bureau came out with a longer statement justifying the general line of the policy which it was pursuing during the last two years, but deigned to admit in the light of the Cominform article "certain errors in dogmatist and sectarian directions" here and there. In an indirect attempt at justifying and offering a plausible explanation of the errors that they were charged with having committed, it was argued that these were but a natural reaction from right-reformism to the opposite direction and "a result of dogmatic over-zealousness" in combating the latter. Thus it came about that party documents "often failed to bring out sharply the colonial character of Indian economy" after the grant of the so-called 'national independence', and to lay proper stress on the anti-imperialist, anti-feudal, national liberationist character of the mass-struggles in the present historical phase. Similarly "a distinction was not always drawn between the big bourgeoisie and other sections of the bourgeoisie" who could become "fellow travellers" of the CPI in "the struggle for national liberation." Rich peasants were in the same manner often lumped together with landlords and which led to the ignoring of the basic fact that "the struggle in rural areas were mainly anti-fedual"and that the class struggle between rich peasant and the agricultural poletariat and poor or middle peasants "were of secondary importance as yet," and soon.

Catching at a straw

We shall have to examine the actual significance and relevance of these self-confessed mistakes of the Ranadivite leadership later on. Here it is enough to note that even in this very unwilling admission of mistakes the CPI Polit-Bureau was practically forced to concede that it had committed errors on every fundamental question at issue with regard to the movement—the definition of the historic phase of the mass struggle, the classes against which it had to be waged and the forces on which it would rely. The only consolation that it could derive, was from its attempt to make out that these mistakes were in the nature of dogmatic over-emphasis here and under-emphasis there. Otherwise it had always been in general agreement with the fundamental outlook represented by the Cominform Editorial. It also sought to hold fast to the 'achievements' of Second Congress Thesis by reiterating the Balabushevich characterisation of it, as "a great step" in the life ofthe party and "the starting point of unleashing the forces of People's liberation struggles in the Indian Union and Pakistan." The Balabushevich-article seemd to be the last thin straw at which it could frantically stretch out its hands, in order to save itself from the impending disgrace. This article was therefore simultaneously published in the main theoretical organ of the party, the Communist, along with the Cominform Editorial article and the statement of the Polit Bureau on the same.

Calcutta thesis goes with the wind!

Leading party-cadres outside the PB and Provincial Executive were however not slow to point out the manifest contradiction between the real ideological and political implications of the Cominform Editorial and the very mild and half-hearted confession of a few dogmatic mistakes of the Polit-Bureau simultaneously with its special pleadings for the tactical line since Second Congress. Hounded by erst-while supporters now turned critics, the ill-fated Polit-Bureau bosses were again compelled to issue another Statement last April, which frankly owns up all sorts of "anti Marxist," "left-sectarian," "opportunist" and even "Trotskyist" mistakes and crimes. This new PB document even admits that it was, as a matter of fact, the basic errors contained in the formulations of the Second Congress Thesis of the party adopted at Calcutta which lay at the root of all subsequent mistakes. Thus the Calcutta Thesis of the CP, which was supposed to have set the "new revolutionary line" for the party two years ago, and was regarded as "a great step in the life of the party" by all foreign fraternal parties at that time, and again by Balabushevich towards the close of the last year, is now in the process of being relegated into the limbo of rejected trash.

Close of Ranadive Period

Joshi, we have seen, was stampeded into admitting his own mistakes in 1948. Now it is the turn of Ranadive. Joshi-ites are gloating over the fact that the 'day of reckoning' and nemesis has come for their humiliators now. Some Adhikery, Dange, Namboodripad or Rajeswar Rao will now be brought forward as the leading figure of this stalinist marionette show in the next phase. The Ranadive peirod is over—its practical usefulness has exhausted in the eyes of the international centre for the present.

Marxism demands an answer!

But every one of us who are interested in the healthy development of a sound and Broad-based revolutionary working class movement in India on the basis of Marxism-Leninism must seriously ponder over these developments. Are the so-called mistakes, blunders, right or left deviations merely the results of the theoretical ineptitude and betrayals of individual leaders—of a Joshi or a Ranadive; or a Browder (USA), Furubotten (Norway), Sanzo Nosaka (Japan) or Konakanishi (Japan)—to take some foreign examples? Or are these persons merely the helpless pawns of some cynical calculus of exigencies extraneous to the fundamental interests of the revolutionary working class movement of their own countries? Every individual member of the CPI who feels that his primary allegiance is to the vast millions of the toiling people of India, to the revolutionary working class, and to the cause of Indian and international Socialist revolution, must find an answer to this question for themselves.

The essence of the Marxist outlook on life—as the founder of Scientific Socialism emphasised long ago—is above all, "critical and revolutionary." Will CP-ers dare to submit the whole history of this self-confessed, collossal political ineptitude of their party as evidenced by the record of the fleeting zig-zag of its errant policies, and the admission of their own leaders to a closer examination from that outlook?

How 'Left' Was 'Left'?

Legend of 'Ultra-leftism'

One of the impressions that is being sought to be created deliberately by Stalinist adherents since the purport of the new cominform directive on Indian Communists became known in this country, is that the political and tactical line which the CPI had been following under Ranadive's leadership since the Calcutta Congress, was as a matter of fact, nothing but a very unrealistic and dogmatic 'ultra-left' line, indistinguishable from that infantile left-comunism, which Lenin condemned so vehemently years ago. In its recoil from the right-reformism of Joshi, the Calcutta Thesis had simply pushed the Party to the other extreme—it is said—in the opposite direction towards left-sectarianism, and eventually led it step by step towards an anti-Marxist Trotskyist position. As such the Ranadive line merited out-right rejection long ago. The CPI Polit-Bureau itself has also come out in a penitent 'self-critical' humility owning up all sorts of 'left'-deviationist mistakes and crimes including Trotskyism. The leading cadres of the party outside Pout-Bureau are similarly engaged in hurling a chorus of accusations against it in the same strain, for having misled the party during these two years and committing all sorts of 'left' and 'ultra-left' sins.

A change to be welcomed?

In the background of the patent futility of the senseless adventurism and the so-called 'militant mass-actions' organised by the Communist Party in these two years, and their disastrous consequences both for the party itself, and for the development of a vigorous and broad-based mass-movement against Congress- capitalist reaction, there will be a general disposition in Marxist and leftist political circles to look with a certain amount of sympathy and approval, upon this criticism of the so-called ultra leftism of Ranadive at the instance of the

Cominform—the highest authoritative Centre of the international Communist movement today.[1] This would be comparable to the general reaction and indignation against the crass reformism of joshi in the past; and the acclamation by certain leftist circles in that back-ground, of the rejection of Joshi-line by the Calcutta Congress of the CPI.

Against both Right-Reformism and Left-Sectarianism

Marxism-Leninism always draws a sharp dividing-line between opportunist right-reformism on the one hand and dogmatic ultra-leftism on the other, both of which often outwardly masquerade as revolutionary phrasemongering. The correct revolutionary strategy and tactics lie along this dividing line and Marxist-Leninists always try through lessons derived from the hard school of practical political experience in the ups and downs of mass-struggles, and also from basic scientific teachings of Marxism to avoid any deviation from this line either to the 'right' or to the 'left.' It is therefore being constantly preached by Stalinist adherents rather assiduously that the new Cominform directive is "a brilliant contribution" to the understanding of the tasks of the present phase of national liberation struggle in India "based upon the correct application of Lenin's and Stalin's teachings." It will undoubtedly help to pull back the Indian communists from the mistakes and misconceived ultra-left policies of the last two and half-years, and enable the CP to take up the correct Marxist- Leninist stand midway between the right-reformism of Joshi and the left-sectarianism of Ranadive, both of which are equally dangerous for the proper development of the revolutionary working class movement.

A Timely warning?

If Joshi had dragged the party far too right in the direction of brazen-faced reformist collaboration with imperialism and the national bourgeoisie in the name of

44

People's War and United Front, Ranadive committed—it is argued—the opposite sort of mistake. In his eagerness to combat the reformism of Joshi he had swung the Party far to the left towards dogmatic left-sectarianism, which is as much a deviation from the correct revolutionary line as right — reformism and is no less harmful. The Cominform Editorial article has therefore come as a timely (!) and much needed warning for the entire party. It will certainly enable leading party cadres and the CPI rank-and-file to fight both against right-reformist and ultra- left mistakes of the past, both against Joshi-ite and Ranadivite deviations, and find their way back to the correct revolutionary strategy and tactics in the true spirit of Marxism.

Or a prelude to Swing-back?

This undue emphasis on the propaganda against the so-called left deviations of Ranadive and the present vehemence of its condemnation may however actually prove nothing but a prelude to a swing back to a subtler form of rightism and a new variety of reformmist class collaborationist line of policy, in the guise of correcting past left-sectarian mistakes—If there is to be an about face towards the right again and a return to open class-collaborationist alliance with certain sections of the Indian bourgeoisie against others, who are in power for the present, or political pressure brought on the present bourgeois ruling circles for a change of governmental policy by utilising the opposition of their discontented and disgruntled rivals, then the present line which was so long confined merely to a policy of barren opposition to the government of the day, must be condemned and thrown overboard as 'ultra-left.' If the sphere of political operation of the party has to be transferred from the arena of opposition to the arena of power-power under the existing order of society and without disturbing its basic class-structure in any way—the denouncement and rejection of the previous policy of unleashing "militant mass actions" and organising "revolutionary onslaughts" against the Nehru Government appears inevitable. If it is felt that the support of considerable sections of the national bourgeoisie could be pressed into service with profit for bringing the party to the forefront again and inducing the Government of the day to reckon with its views, then some theoretical plea must be discovered for an alliance with them. All indirect or direct references to fundamental social change; or to the imminence of a Socialist revolution and the overthrow of capitalism must in that case also be eschewed demonstratively. The theoretical ground for this could be most conveniently cleared with an apparent air of plausibility about it, by rejecting the existing tactical line of the party as left deviationist and fundamentally misconceived.

A 'relative' shift only!

A relative shift to the right from a tactical line which has somehow moved far "too left" is always justifiable from the point of view of Marxism and commonsense [Marxism is, as a matter of fact, nothing but concentrated revolutionary realism and common sense]. If the Ranadive line and the Calcutta Thesis can be proved to have been really ultra-left then its summary rejection and the subsequent adoption of an open class-collaborationist policy would be provided with the required ideological and theoretical sanction in the minds of the rank-and-file. But this new variant of right-reformism could still be distinguished from old "Joshi-ite right-reformism" by calling it the scientific Lenin- Stalin Bolshevik line, which is opposed both to deviations on the left as well as those on the right. It would thus be still possible to characterise the new right about-turn as a genuine 'left' stand, and a correct revolutionary Marxist-Leninist stand at that, sharply demarcated from the Ranadivite 'ultra-left' but formally distinguished at the same time from the officially condemned, tarred and feathered Joshi-ite ultra-right. That is the genesis of the legend of Ranadive's 'ultra-leftism.'

No back-to-Joshi-line

In other words the CPI is now required by the international Stalinist leadership—the CPSU and the Cominforin i.e., —for reasons of their own, to make a turn to the right again. But the fact has to be kept carefully concealed from the view of the average rank-and-file workers of the party. They must continue to believe that they are still in the 'left,' but not the wrong kind left, the ultra-left. If the party is again apparently moving to the right, that is nothing but a relative shift-back from a left-deviationist line of policy to the correct revolutionary Marxist-Leninist policy, holding delicate balance between left-sectarianism and right-reformism. It must not be confused with Joshi's reformism which even Joshi himself has condemned unreservedly. It is not to be a back-to- Joshi policy. The Cominform article actually helps the CPI, it is contended, to fight both right-reformism and ultra-leftism, and in the immediate context serves to correct Ranadive's left-sectarian mistakes especially. As always, the party is again enabled to find its way back to the 'correct' 'revolutionary' strategy and tactics. When it is a question of having committed a mistake it is always a Browder, a Tito, a Joshi or Nosaka, a Furubotten and a Sharkey on the right, or a Nakanishi Shiga, Miyamoto and Ranadive on the left, who are primarily responsible.[2] The international leadership-the CPSU and its mouthpiece the Cominform, are of course always correct, always infallible and above reproach.

Leftism or Adventurism?

The legend of the so-called "leftism" or "ultra-leftism" of Ranadive needs to be examined therefore a bit more closely. Was the Ranadive line as formulated by the Calcutta Thesis and its subsequent elaborations by the CPI Polit-Bureau, politically a 'left' line at all? How much 'left' was Ranadive's ultra-leftism really? Leftism as the expression of a defined political and ideological trend in the working class emancipation movement must be sharply distinguised from that type of adventurist terrorist armed actions totally divorced from any broad-based political support from the masses, which was indulged in by the CPI during the course of past two years. As a matter of fact these are rather the expressions of a basic political reformism and opportunism which shrinks, in the words of Lenin from "the persistent, patient and sustained work of educating the masses in the spirit of class- consciousness even in the most un-inspiring humdrum days of bourgeois-constitutional Shipov bliss." It relies in the main on sharp shooting pressure tactics to gain its immediate, but very limited, political objectives against the government of the day without undermining it fundamentally.

Adventurism in nine cases out of ten is nothing but the direct outcome of this reformism and an anti-working class, anti- people political opportunism. It has nothing in common with 'leftism' on the political and ideological plane which aims at fundamental social and political transformation by political mass- action and the organised strength of the masses under the leadership of the working class.

Seizure-of-Power by acid-bulbs?

In the recent self-critical documents of the CPI Polit-Bureau, as well as in the adverse criticism of the Polit-Bureau by ex- Ranadivites outside, who have now suddenly become very much aware of the 'criminal' lapses of the Ranadive line, there is a general tendency to explain away the adventurism of the past two years by reference to the so-called "leftism" or 'ultra-leftism" of the Calcutta Thesis and that of the subsequent theoretical formula- tions on 'Strategy and Tactics etc., by the Polit-Bureau. "Any one who commits mistakes regarding the nature of revolution is bound to commit mistakes regarding concrete revolutionary tasks"—it has been said in the one of these self-critical documents (Draft Statement prepared by the CPI. PB for the new Central Committee)—as if the tactics of acid-bulb throwing, tram-burning and armed raids on isolated police out-posts in outlying rural areas, were the results of Ranadive's misconceptions as to the nature of the Indian Revolution! Because Ranadive failed to realise that India is still 'a colonial country' under foreign imperialist domination (so the Stalinists contend, since the publication of the Cominforni Editorial), and that the new phase of Indian revolution is still mainly an anti-feudal anti-imperialist bourgeois-democratic revolution, and not an anti-capitalist Socialist one, he became confused himself and misled the party to these adventurist tactics! It is sometimes also argued that Ranadivite adventurism was due to his misunderstandings about the present tactical stage of the Indian revolution and mistaking it for the stage of seizure of power, corresponding to something like the intervening months between February and October 1917 in Russia—the midway phase between the February and October Revolutions[3] while as a matter of fact, seizure of power—a Socialist seizure of power for the matter of that, was far off as yet—as if a Socialist seizure of power is ever effected by these tactics!

Lenin on 'Seizure-of-power' struggles

Both Ranadive himself and his recent critics must have known however—and there is no reason to suppose that they were unacquainted with the fact—that even while actually standing midway between February and October, and urging the Bolshevik Party to the slogan of "All Power to the Soviets" in terms of a Socialist seizure-of-power, Lenin defined the main task of the Bolsheviks as one of "patiently explaining" before the masses the class character of the bourgeois government and the class significance of the problems that confronted them. Reporting on the political situation of Russia in May, 1917 he emphasised clearly that:

To speak of civil war before people have come to realise the need for it, is undoubtedly to fall in Blanquism. We are for a civil war aged by a class conscious proletariat at the head of the people. Only he can be over thrown who is known to the people as a despot The masses are influenced by tradition and deception. They still lack political experience. Therefore our task is patient explaining...

"To speak of violence now" said Lenin then, beyond any scope of misunderstanding, "is pure nonsense", and continued further:

The masses of our population have never been Socialists. They have not the slightest conception of Socialism, they are just awakening to political life. But their class consciousness is growing and broadening with extraordinary rapidity.

One must know how... to approach them with explanations.

One must know how to look from the Marxist standpoint which says that the imperialist war would turn into civil war, as a result of objective conditions not as a result of subjective desires.

He admonished the Bolsheviks against regarding the task of "patiently explaining" as nothing but a bloodless, colourless, humdrum work and said :

This may appear to be 'nothing more' than mere propaganda work, but in reality it is extremely revolutionary practical work; for there is no advance for a revolution that has come to a standstill, that has choked itself with phrases, not because of external circumstances, not because of the violence of the bourgeosie, but because of naive trust of the masses. Tasks of the Proletariat, Selected Works, pp 30-31.

And here follows the concrete programme which Lenin set forth before his party:

Only by combating this naive trust (and one can combat it only ideologically, by comradely persuasion, by pointing to the lessons of experience can we escape the prevailing orgy of phrase-mongering and make real progress in stimulating class consciousness both of the proletariat and of the masses in general, as well as stimulating determined initiative in various localities... for the realisation, development and consolidation of their democratic liberties.

No comment is required on these clear-cut and unambiguous directives.

Revolutionary Violence vs. Adventurism

If Lenin could say this after the formation of the Soviets and the overthrow of the Czar, under conditions when side by side with Govemement of the bourgeoisie emerged the 'dual power of the Workers' Pesants' and Soldiers' Soviets (a concrete realisation of the Democratic Dictatorship of the Proletariat and Peasantry), when elemental mass-forces were on the move, consciously intervening in the affairs of the state, it is more than obvious that time for any form of violent or armed action, (not to speak of the type of adventurist-terroristic armed action completely divorced from aiy conceivable contact with the political consciousness of the masses, in which the CPI indulged), was far remote from the conditions of our country. By no stretch of imagination it could be conceived as called for by the objective historic situation or the level of mass-consciousness obtaining in India any time after 1948. Revolutionary Marxism certainly does not rule out violence, force or armed action as a method of social and political transformation. But it is always violence consciously employed by the armed people, themselves, on behalf of the overwhelming majority of the people against the minority of capitalists and other exploiters who monopolise power, with a clearly defined political objective in view viz; the overthrow of the rule of these capitalists and exploiters and the establishment, in its place, of the rule of the toiling people headed by working class "for civil war, but for a civil war waged by a class

51

conscious proletariat"—that is the irrevocably fundamental standpoint of Marxism-Leninism about seizure-of-power struggles.

Ignorance, or a Deliberate tactical move?

There is no reason to suppose, as we have already indicated, that Ranadive or the CPI leadership were unacquainted with these cardinal principles of armed action or seizure-of-power struggles as envisaged by Marxism-Leninism. The type of armed action to which the CPI resorted in the name of seizure-of-power struggles were so much removed from any living contact with the actual needs or consciousness of the masses (except to a certain extent in Telengana in Hyderabad, the Kakdwip village in the Sundarban areas of West Bengal and the tribal Hajong area in the Garo Hills all of which lie in very inaccessible and outlying parts of the country and are separated by hundreds and thousands of miles from each other), were so frivolously and flimsily conceived and the inadequateness of the preparation of the mass-front organisations and the party for withstanding the recoil of these actions were so very marked— that even a very ultra-left 'revolutionary' doctrinaire like a Ranadive, or a Bhowani Sen, could not be supposed as entertaining the least illusion about these actions developing, into, or ever leading to the overthrow of the existing government and to seizure of power by any far chance. As a matter of fact the Polit-Bureau of the CPI could not keep their eyes altogether shut to the hard reality that in the major part of this vast country the state of organisation and political consciousness of the people had not yet reached the stage of armed seizure-of-power struggles. It could not be otherwise in a colonial country where the national bourgeoisie had just come to power on the crest a national mass-upsurge by utilising their vantage position in the leadership of the national mass-movement to drive a bargaining deal with foreign imperialism behind the backs of the masses.

State of mass-consciousness in India

The level of consciousness and organisation of the masses proved absolutely inadequate, it must not be forgetten, to prevent the ignominious compromise between imperialism and the native bourgeoisie against the vital interests of the nation and the toiling people. The minds of the masses were still steeped deep in fond illusions about the very same bourgeois national leaders who had come to power by betraying them. The process of disillusionment had of-course begun on the morrow of the "transfer of power"; and new mass-movements of profound historical significance had started. The masses had begun to awake to the new consciousness of their own independent class interests and class demands. They had also naturally begun to judge their 'trusted national leaders' and their national government in terms of these demands. But nevertheless in 1948-49, it was no more than the first beginnings of the new stirring amongst the common people and the opening out of a new phase of mass-struggles which would henceforth be directly and primarily directed against the ruling bourgeoisie and the so-called 'national' government.

Two major facts

But in spite of this, the overall political situation in the country was however still patently dominated by two major facts:

(1) a temporary stabilisation of the political power of the national bourgeoisie as the new ruling-class in collusion with and backing of foreign imperialism, and their close alliance with native feudal vested interests;

and (2), the inevitably imperfect and gradual process of the disillusionment of the masses, and lack of self-confidence in their minds about strength of their own class-organisations.

Polit-Bureau admits! 'Telengana Way' cum Deputations

The result was, as the Polit-Bareau was forced to admit, that the level of consciousness of the workers and peasants in most parts of the country, even in class-organisations under direct CPI leadership and control, did not rise as yet above filing cases before governement Tribunals, and pressing their minimum economic demands, petition in hand, before the authorities. "We (i.e., the CPI) still participate in Parliaments, lead deputations and demonstrations, appear before Industrial Tribunals in trade disputes, participate in Tripartite (Govt. Employer-Employee) Conferences etc., —the CPI. Polit Bureau wrote in their lengthy disquisition on "Strategy and Tactics" about the middle of last year (see Communist No. 4.1949). "We can't get away"—it was frankly owned up "from the most elementary forms of struggle" .... "Life is such that the Party which wields arms in Telengana, files cases before Industrial tribunals in Bombay and Calcutta"!

"Uneven development"!

The Irony of combining the 'Telengana Way' slogan with timidly filing workers' cases before Industrial Tribunals did not escape the notice of the Pout-Bureau altogether. But this was put down in the Report on "Strategy and Tactics" to the "uneven development of the consciousness of the masses." It was also recognised that the "bourgeoisie still possessed great influence in the country." The situation was "full of revolutionary possibilities", but unfortunately the masses were not "learning and moving with uniform consciousness." It was all due to the inertness of the masses! The masses had to be spurred into action somehow and enabled to. get over their passiveness. This could only be done under the circumstances, by the party intself coming forward to take up the initiative and launch militant struggles on its own account. "Just because it is a revolutionary period the most elementary struggles (Petition-filing before Industrial Tribunals?) will set in motion forces which enable the masses to overcome their present consciousness"—it was expected, and rapidly lead them take up the most advanced forms of struggle! Apparently Ranadive and his colleagues seemed to have little doubts about that.

Lenin's caution deliberately ignored

In the background of the objective historic possibility of the miscarriage of the democratic revolution in Russia (1905), and the danger of an imperialist-bourgeois alliance coming to power owing to the weakness and the inadequate level of preparation and conciousness of the masses, Lenin uttered long ago the supreme revolutionary caution that it will be necessary "or continue in the *persistent, patient, sustained* work of educating the proletariat in the spirit of class-consciousness and to proceed along a thorny, hard and long, but familiar and beaten trail" (Two Tactics Selected Works pp. 312-3). This caution was however totally ignored. In order to rouse the party rank-and-file to militant mass actions and armed struggles (which earned praises from men like Balabushevich and others) it was constantly dinned into their ears 'that the situation is full of revolutionary possibilities,' and once the party starts fighting and puts the issues of political power squarely before the masses, they would automatically begin to learn with astonishing rapidity. It was not a question of masses learning by their own experience; or the party undertaking to explain patiently to the masses the political class significance of that experience, and leading them step by step through the ups and downs of their actual struggles to higher levels of consciousness and organised action on which Lenin emphasised in 1917. It was rather a case of "start-fight-the-masses-will follow" sort of complacence which has always provided the main argument for Blanquism and all kinds of fire brand adventurism. "The *objective of overthrowing the bourgeoisie*"combined with the "existence of a *revolutionary period* and rapidly moving revolutionary developments", it was accordingly deduced, "compels resort to militant and revolutionary forms of struggle."

"Hence *strikes, agrarians struggles, general strikes, political strikes,* rising to higher forms of struggle and to a general rising" such are the forms of struggle that flow from the situation.[4] So the party must, be prepared to use the most elementary forms of struggle with the "highest and most advanced forms," seizure- of-power struggles and armed insurrections—"with the one object of rapidly bringing the masses to the point at which they themselves will echo the party's cry of ending the government" ('On Strategy and Tactics').

Job-chart of Stalinist power-politics

The masses of course did not echo the CPI slogans. It was rather the CPI which got itself increasingly isolated day by day from the masses. But that hardly deterred the CPI leadership. They were faithfully following the job-chart with 'which they were briefed in the overall plan of "resistance to the anti-Soviet Anglo- American imperialist plans of aggression along every line." The realities ofthe objective historical situation in India, the alignment of class forces here or the level of consciousness and organisation of the major sections of the Indian toiling people were factors of secondary importance so far as the CPI were concerned. The major objective was to be engaged in some sort of trouble-raising in this country, in common with Communist movements elsewhere in Asia, so as to create the impression that a revolution was breaking out, that a mass-upsurge had begun in India and the govenrment of the Congress bourgeoisie, which had come to power with Anglo American backing and slavishly toeing the anti Soviet Anglo-American line of foreign policy, was going to crumble down in no time. If the masses could not be mobilised for that purpose owing to "the uneven development of their consciousness", then the party rank-file must be inspired to do the job with the exhortation that as soon as they start fighting the masses will follow. Only in this way can we explain Ranadive's arguments in favour the necessity of "combining the most elementary with the most advanced forms of struggle" and resorting to armed seizure- of-power struggles on the plea of "rapidly moving revolutionary developments in a revolution-period." Because only in this way he could at least make the party rank-and-files move. He did the best-it must be conceded—that he could, and was 'expected' to do under the circumstances.

Notes

1. It has already induced one of the leading left parties of Western India, the Maharastra peasant's and Worker's Party (Shctkari Icamgar Paksha) to come out with a statement welcoming the new Cominform directive and proclaiming its political allegiance to the Cominform Centre while vehemently criticising the CPI at the same time for its 'left- sectarianism' and 'adventurism.' Coming close on the publication of Mr. P.C. Joshis' letter to foreign communist Parties against Ranadive (Views, No. 1.) the declaration of the SKP caused a certain amount of political flutter both in this country and abroad, and gave currency to the report that a rival Communist Party was being formed in India. The leader of the MSKP, Mr. S. S. More has denied this subsequently.

2. Browder was the former leader of the US Communist Party till 1946 and was expelled from the party like Joshi on the charge of right-reformism. Nosaka, Eunibotlen and Sharkey have been denounced, one time or other, as right-deviationist in Japan, Norway and Australia. Nosaka and Sharkey have again been put on grace. Furubotten has broken with CPN and formed his own party. Nakanishi Shiga and Miyamoto were recently condemned by the CP. Japan on charges of left-deviation when they came out with too outspoken a criticism of the Nosaka-line and for advocating a more militant class-struggle programme without taking account that Nosaka—a close friend of Mao Tse-tung-had been restored to favour again. Ranadive has to go for having criticised Mao; his Japanese counterpart for falling foul with Mao's friend on being misled initially by Cominform criticism of the latter.

The original Cominform charge-sheet against Tito contained indictment, it should be noted, both on counts of right and left deviations. He is now of course no more a 'deviationist' merely, but a full-fledged "Fascist hireling" in the pay of US imperialism! The main differences with which Sharkey have been involved, concern the Communist Party of Great Britain and certain leaders of CP, France and Italy, whom he charged with right-deviationism. He in his turn has been accused of Browderism and Titoism!

3. In December 1948 the CPI Polit-Bureau had actually defined the present phase of Indian revolution as "mixed"—comparable partly to February and partly to October.

4. The short hand formula for this which, according to the Calcutta District Committee of the Party, was handed to the rank-and file about this time, runs thus— surround the factory management and the employers—after 'surrounding' start 'beating'—from 'beating' to 'strike'—from 'strike' to a 'procession of the armed people'—from 'armed procession' to 'street-barricades', 'violent clashes' and 'armed

insurrection' for seizure of power." It was all as easy as that!

A Matter of Foreign Policy

'Without illusions'

It is patently absurd to suggest, as is being done by leading Stalinist circles in course of 'critical, self-critical' analysis of their recent mistakes in the light of Cominform Editorial, that the non-sensical adventurist tactics of struggle to which the CPI resorted since the Calcutta Congress had any relations with Ranadive's conception of the inter-relation between the so-called People's Democratic Revolution and the Socialist Revolution, or with his definition of the character of the present phase of revolution in India as a national democratic or Socialist one. Neither did it have. any logical or ideological relation with the slogan of Socialist seizure of power. We have to note firstly that in spite of his attempts to pass on Stalinist People's Democratic reformism as a kind of near-Socialism before CPI rank-and-file and the masses, Ranadive never raised the slogan of Socialist revolution as the immediate historic object of the party. In fact he never forgot to emphasise that the coming phase of revolution in this country would clearly take the character of a People's Democratic Revolution immediately, and will not definitely be a Socialist one. He, of course, wanted to prove at the same time, more as a sop to the militant Socialist covictions of the party rank-and-file, that this revolution-though called 'democratic' would not be like the old type of bourgeois-democratic revolutions. State power in a People's Democracy would be wielded by the workers, peasants and other toilers, the common people, under the leadership of the working-class, and not by capitalists, landlords and other vested interests as in bourgeois-democracy. It would therefore quickly pass-over into Socialism; although it was not a Socialist revolution directly in the immediate present.[1] Secondly, as we have seen above, there is no reason to suppose that in spite of his call for a seizure-of-power struggle, he ever had any illusions about the actual level of consciousness of the masses or their organisation being prepared for such a struggle.

"He had to give the call"

But nevertheless he had to give the call for such a struggle, because only in this way he could ideologically inspire the rank-and-file to engage in hit-and-run armed struggles against the Congress government, which he was pursuaded to think, would be the easiest of way of making that government feel the weight of CPI against its pro-Anglo-American foreign policy. If one needs to be convinced of this, he has only refer to the CPI polit Bureau's statement on the "Fight Against War Danger" which was published simultaneously 'along with the allegedly "Left- Sectarian" Report on "Strategy and Tactics" which is supposed to have given the call for seizure-of-power struggles.

A matter of Foreign Policy

"To day when the world bourgeoisie is making an insane drive for the war, when unknown to the Indian people the *treacherous Indian bourgeoisie is conspiring with imperialism for an anti-Soviet War "*—argued the PB document "On War Danger" failure to isolate, to fight the bourgeoisie…constitute a danger and a menace." Every effort must be made to expose, isolate and run down the bourgeoisie and its foreign policy; and the best way to do this would be the method of combining loud 'vocal' propaganda against the India Government's 'collaborationist' foreign policy with the method of "fight" or launching offensives against the governments. The real meaning of the exhortations in the statement on "Strategy and Tactics" about "the necessity of combining the most advanced and elementary forms of struggle—with the one object of bringing the masses to the point at which they themselves will echo the party's cry for ending the government"—can only be understood in this context. Only by this means would it be possible to make India government realise that its support to anti-soviet war-mongering policies of Anglo-America would not be tolerated by the masses, the working class, and at least by the CPI.

'Nehru must join the Soviet Camp.'

The statement on the "Fight against war Danger" accordingly emphasises the imperative necessity of combining the "fight against the bourgeoisie" with the "exposure of the India Government's anti-Soviet and pro-Anglo-American foreign policy" with the campaign to explain to the people "how the Soviet Union is the real defender of the Sovereignty of all nations." It was especially urgent, it was pointed out, to raise the demand that India should enter into economic and other agreements with the Soviet Union (see pp. 90-96, *The Communist,* No. 4; 1949). Pacts with the Soviet "would develop the economic strength of the nation and keep national sovereignty inviolable." And, although it was true, there was no real semblance of independence and national sovereignty in India at present in the opinion of the CPI, the party must carry on a vigorous propaganda "for defending them;" and for the view that "the country would be enabled to defend its independence and national sovereignty only by allying itself with the Soviet and democratic anti-imperialist bloc." If we care to bear in mind the context of the post-war break up of Anglo-

US-Soviet alliance in this connection and the theory of the division of the world into "two camps" as set forth by Zhdanov in his inaugural Cominform speech, we would have no difficulty in appreciating the object that CPI hit-and-run struggles against the Congress Government (glorified as seizure-of-power actions) had in view. Though couched in zingle-zingle 're-revolutionary' phraseology of an imminent upsurge, political strikes, general rising etc. these had no relation even in the allegedly 'ultra-left' consciousness of the Ranadivite leadership with any immediate practical possibility for actual 'seizure of power,' whether 'democratic' or Socialist. Its only purpose in view was to mobilise immature petty bourgeois left-revolutionism of the youthful rank- and-file for hit-and-run struggle against the Congress government as a part of the international pressure-tactics of Stalinism, in the game of Soviet power-rivalry with the Anglo-American bloc. It was principally because of this that the "active participation" 'of students and lower strata of the petty-bourgeoisie "in the militant political actions taking place under the leadership of the CPJ" did not fail to receive due kudos from Soviet propagandists like Balabushevich till the other day. The news of the pro-Soviet Resolution of Firozabad Peace Rally was guarantee enough that the "mass political actions" undertaken by the CPI was proceeding on "truly correct" and "revolutionary" lines and that the programme of the party "expressed the aspirations and hopes of Indian people"! [2]

Notes:

1. This was the leading strain of the entire political stand of the CPI from 1948 to 1950, beginning from the Calcutta Thesis right up to Polit-Bureau dissertations on 'People's Democracy' (Dec. 1948-January 1949) and 'Strategy and Tactics' (June-July, 1949). Everybody, including the Ranadivite Polit-Bureau itself is now up in arms against Ranadive's definition of People's Democratic Revolution as "the democratic revolution which is more than ever interlaced with the Socialist revolution in each country and the world" and of its tasks in terms of "the completion of the tasks of democratic revolution and the simultaneous building up of Socialism." This is now being condemned as a Trotskyist and ultra-left formulation. But nobody dared to contradict Ranadive in 1948 and early 1949 when he cited the views of Zhdanov and the veteran Kusinen (*New Times*), September 1948, in support of his definition.

Stalinist People's Democracy has in fact so many different and mutually contradictory definitions that it is dangerous to stick to any one of these for long without being charged with some sort of left or right deviation. The Soviet publicist Sokolov defined the achievements of People's Democracy in terms of the completion of the tasks of bourgeois democratic revolution, and demarcated them sharply from the socialist revolution or the dictatorship of the proletariat. Eugene Varga, and then Kusinen again, defined it as an intermediate transition stage between capitalism and Socialism. Kuzmihov, editor of the CPSU theoretical organ, the *Bolshevik* quoted Lenin to deny that there could be any such intermediate stage. Zhdanov defined it as a 'new type' of state which carries through "progressive democratic reforms such as bourgeois-democracy is no longer capable of effecting," but which simultaneously "paves the way for entry on to the path of Socialist development." After the revolt of Tito and his allegations against CPSU and the Cominform about obstructing the programme of Socialist industrialiation in Yugoslavia, Dimitrov of Bulgaria, Beirut and Hilary Minc of Poland, and others however came out with a new definition of

People's Democracy as a "specific variegated form of Socialist revolution and the Dictatorship of the Proletariat" achieved "without the employment of largescale violence and anti-capitalist civil war under the guidance and direct help from the Soviet Union." Contrasted with this stand the original formulation of People's Democratic revolution by Mao Tse-Tung of China as "an anti-imperialist and anti feudal revolution only" and which was definitely not an anti-capitalist or Socialist revolution. In China atleast, he seems to think "capitalism will have to be allowed to continue for a longtime to come." The Cominform leadership now seems to approve the Mao-version of People's Democracy for India also, and for Asian countries in general. The Ranadive formulation stood midway between those of Mao and Dimitrov Beirut People's Democracy is either Socialism or no-Socialism. As a true Stalinist dialectician Ranadive refused to accept this hard and fast either-or definition and regarded it safer to follow undisputed authorities like Zhdanov and Kusinen in linking up Socialism with People's Democracy as a sequel, as something evolving out of it inevitably. Only in this way he could sell People's Democracy to Marxist Public opinion and to his rank-and-file. He forgot perhaps that different authorities and different definitions of the same phenomenon are kept reserved in the Stalinist pantry to suit different political objectives in different contexts. The Zhdanov-Kusinen-Ranadive thesis of People's Democracy now has lost its usefulness so far India is concerned after having served its purpose for the last two years. Ranadive has now to make kow-tows before Mao. Unfortunately for him that does not save him. He must also beat his breast, tear hairs from his head and brand himself as a 'left-opportunist' & 'Trotskyist' for the crime of having echoed Zhdanov & Kusinen and linking up Socialism with People's Democracy. It is now being asserted that Ranadive "revised Zhdanov's formulation about new-democracy" and did not distinguish between People's Democracy in an advanced capitalist country and People's Democracy in a colonial country" (Draft Resolution for Central Committee May, 1950). But it is conveniently forgotten that Zhdanov's definition specifically related to East-European new-democratic republics, which with the exception of Czechoslovakia other countries have always been classified as countries of a very back ward capitalist development and as satellite or dependent states underforeign imperialist hegemony. Yet Ranadive dared not identify itwith Socialism Dimitrov-Beirut-Mine fashion! One can only wonder 'whom to follow in this maze of self-contradictions'! And then, what is meant by People's Democracy in advanced capitalist countries precisely? Does it mean that the objective of Socialist revolution does not hold good for advanced capitalist countries even? As a matter of fact that is the view of the international Stalinist movement under the influence of the theories of "Socialism in a single country" and "Peaceful co-existence of Socialism and Capitalism side by side."

2. It is significant that somehow or other this particular document of the Randive period—the PB. Report "On the Fight against War Danger" has escaped adverse self-critical comments in CPI circles. One hardly needs wonder why. Its basic content somehow provides the sheet-anchor of Stalinist strategy in India.

The New Enlightenment

Those two potent paragraphs!

In order to judge the correctness or otherwise of the charges brought against Ranadive on various counts of left-Sectarian deviation and the political significance of those charges it will be necessary to discuss at-length the theoretical implications of the new line which has been suggested to the CPI by the new Cominform directive.

This directive came in the form of a two column Editorial article in the Cominform weekly *"For a Lasting Peace, For a People's Democracy"* (January 27, 1950) entitled 'Mighty Advance of the National Liberation Movement in the Colonial and Dependent Countries.! This article made a passing reference in two short paragraphs to the post-war political situation in India after the imposition of the Mountbatten Plan of 'sham independence'and the tasks confronting the Indian communists in that context. Apparently the article was nothing but an usual disquisition on the unprecedented sweep and scope of colonial national liberation movements in the post-war internatinal situation, and the conditions of its success in China and other Asian countries. It contained, as we have mentioned earlier, no adverse criticism of the line of policy which was being actually followed in this country by the CPI for the last two years under the leadership of Ranadive, or of the political thesis of the Calcutta Congress which provided the theoretical background for that line. But in spite of that these two short paragraphs were powerful enough to upset the entire Indian Communist Party and its organisational and political activities. It at once threw the CPI Polit-Bureau in confusion and unleashed a spate of 'self-critical' invectives and insults against the latter from all and sundry. After a few feeble attempts at self-justification and to salvage of some parts at least its 'hither-to-correct' revolutionary line of programme and also to save its

65

political 'face', the Polit-Bureau itself was ultimately forced to come out in contrite self condemnation of all sorts 'deviations', 'criminal mistakes', and 'lapses' that were committed. In the background of the high-powered revelation vouched in these two paragraphs the whole party has now after two years come to realise that it was the fundamentally mistaken theoretical formulations of the Calcutta Thesis which lay at the root of these colossal tactical mistakes, deviations and lapses. The Calcutta Thesis which was adopted by the entire Party Congress with loud acclamations and 'hails' as the only *correct revolutionary* line, 'doing *honour* 'to the party rank-and-file and its leadership, is now thrown overboard at a stroke of the pen. It is certain that Ranadive and his Polit-Boreau who were responsible for leading the party these two and half years will also have to go. 'The day of reckoning' has come for Ranadive as P.C. Joshi had been crusing and hoping these two years. The two brief paragraphs of the Cominform Editorial were potent enough to bring about all this and close the two-year chapter in the history of the party with a bang. The Zhdanov speech to the inaugural Cominform Conference had served the notice for quit on Joshi. The Cominform Editorial serves a similar notice on Ranadive. Exit Randive! Enter Rajeswar Rao or someone else who will be pliable enough and adaptative enough to uphold the line of the Cominform directive and switch the party to the position now required by the international leadership. It goes without saying that all these are bound to be the effects of those two brief paragraphs of the Cominform Editorial.

What the Cominform Directive actually said

But we are here more concerned with its Political implications.The two aforementioned paragraphs of the Comminform article which specifically refer to India and the tasks of Indian Communists read thus:

The mass movement of the peoples in colonies and semi colonies, the movement that unfolded after the war and developed into an armed struggle, forced the British imperialists to make a tactical retreat. A sham indepen- dence was bestowed on India. But the interests of British imperialism remain 'sacred and inviolable. The Mountbattens have departed but British imperialism remains, and octopus-like grips India in its bloody tentacles.

In these conditions the task of Indian Communists, drawing on the experience of national liberation movement in China and other countries, is naturally', to strengthen the alliance of the working class with all the peasantry, to fight for the introduction of urgently needed agrarian reform-on the basis of the common struggle for freedom and national independence of their country, against Anglo-American imperialists oppressing it and against the reactionary big bourgeoisie and the feudal princes collaborating with them-to unite all classes, parties, group and organisations willing to defend the national independence and freedom of India.

Follow the China Way!

The reference to the necessity of "drawing on the experience of the national liberation movement in China" was specially significant in view of the bitter criticism made by Ranadivite Polit- Bureau against certain aspects of the line of policy of the Chinese Communist Party and Mao Tse-Tung. It was specifically stated earlier in the article that:

"The victory of the Chinese people is of enormous significance in strengthening the national liberation struggle in the colonial and dependent countries."

The view expressed by the Chinese Communist leader Liu ShaoChi in his opening speech to the Trade Union Conference of Asian and Australasian countries in Peking (November, 1949) about conditions of the victory of the Chinese People's revolution and his statement that—

"The path taken by the Chinese people-is the path that

67

should be taken by the people of many colonial and dependent countries in their struggle for national independence and people's democracy"-was quoted with special approval.[1] The lessons of the experience of Chinese people's liberation struggle, which was led by the Communist Party of China and to which the attention of Indian communists were specially drawn, was summed up in the following terms:

The experience of the victorious national liberation struggle of the Chinese people teaches that the working class must unite with all classes, parties and group and organisations willing to fight the imperialists and their hirelings and to form a broad, nation-wide front, headed by the Working class and its vanguard, the Communist Party.

A 'Nation-Wide United Front'

This provides the political premise on the basis of which the liberation struggle in India must proceed and the CPI was in effect asked to recast its tactics on that basis, on the Chinese pattern of a nation-wide united front with all classes, parties, groups and organisations willing to fight the imperialists and their hirelings. From the point of view of its fundamental political and theoretical implications it was an order to a return to the previous policy of United National Front which held the field from 1936 onwards with minor changes that were necessitated by the tactical retreat of British imperialism and the practical consequences of the Mountbatten Plan. And in order to make sure that CPI ranks do not misunderstand their day-to day tactical tasks, it was again reiterated with emphasis after the two above mentioned specific references to India that:

The Communist Parties, trade unions and all democratic organisations in the Colonial and dependent countries should rally the working people and all progressive forces, daily expose the colonising plans of foreign imperialists and the treacherous anti-popular role of reaction which collaborates with the imperialists.

68

Unity above all

Unity with all progressive democratic forces, rallying of the working sections of the people, peasants, workers, Lower-middle-classes, intellectuals along with people of all other classes (including the 'national bourgeoisie') who are against imperialism and the exposure of colonising plans of foreign imperialists and the role of native collaborators of imperialism-these were the two main political tasks which are set forth by the Cominform Centre to the CPI ranks beyond which it must not go for the present. This naturally meant in the first instance peremptory order to the party to cease the type of "militant mass-action" participated by students and other petty-bourgeois elements, which had earned compliments from Comrade Balabushevich, forthwith. The tactics of "combining the most elementary forms of struggle with the most advanced ones, "of wielding arms in the "Telengana way" and arguing workers' petitions before Industrial Tribunals in Bombay and Calcutta and trying to rush the masses by hurrah methods "to the point where they will echo the party's cry for ending the Government," the tactics of "general rising and seizure- of-power struggles" etc., must stop and give place to the struggle for unity and collaboration with all *progressive democratic* forces and *political exposure* of imperialists and their collaborators.

Treat the national-bourgeoisie as an ally!

In the background of the emphasis laid on the tactics of unity with all progressive classes, parties, groups and organisations etc., and on the necessity of drawing upon the experiences of the successful national liberation movement in China under the leadership of Chinese Communists, the Cominform directive was also a clear pointer to the CPI for revising their policy of opposition to the national bourgeoisie as a whole and coming out openly for uniting them, excluding the big-bourgeoisie of course who were collaborating. As Mao Tse-

69

tung had pointed out long before, the People's Democratic Revolution was an *anti-imperialist and anti- feudal* revolution only and definitely *not an anti-capitalist* one. Hence the Chinese Communists "were far from being unsympathetic to capitalism actually promoted its development." All Chinese Communist leaders from Mao. to Liu Shao-Chi and Li Li-San were emphatic that one of the major conditions for the success of Chinese Communist Party in establishing its leadership in the national liberation movement and carrying that movement to victory lay in the fact that "it found the correct policy in dealing with *national bourgeoisie,* differentiating the national bourgeoisie which opposed imperialism from the big bourgeoisie who have capitulated to imperialism, not opposing the national bourgeoisie as a national enemy, but treating it as an ally" (Li Li-San, Speech to TUCAA; Peking Nov. 1949). The CPI were now in effect told to do the same thing in India. This was the concrete meaning of the tactics of the 'broad nation-wide united front with all classes, parties' etc., which was suggested in the Cominform directive. Liberation Armies?

What was the view expressed in the Cominform Editorial- it may be asked here about armed struggles and the formation of Liberation Armies without the help of which the Chinese people's liberation movement could not certainly have achieved the phenomenal success which it has won and come to power? Were such struggles and the organisation of people's Liberation Armies to be undertaken in India also? No direct answer was given to the question with any special reference to India. It was only remarked as a bare statement of fact that:

A decisive condition for the victorious outcome of the national-liberation struggle is the formation, when the necessary internal conditions allow for it, of people's liberation armies under the leadership of Communist Party;

and

that the example of China, Viet Nam, Malaya and other countries show, armed struggle is now becoming the main form of struggle in many colonial and dependent countries.

Not yet the time in India

But no mention was made of India amongst countries where internal conditions for the formation of National Liberation Armies and for the commencement of armed struggle against imperialists and their collaborators had been reached. China, Viet Nam, Malaya, South Korea, Philippines, Indonesia and even Burma were specifically mentioned.[2]

But absolutely no reference was made to the wielding of arms in Telengana, Kakdwip and Hajong areas in this country of which the CPI Pout-Bureau boasted so much. Balabushevich had called the Telengana armed struggle, "the harbinger of Indian agrarian revolution and 'the most important content of the national liberation struggle' which was being led by the CPI. But not so the Cominform Editorial Board.

First things first

In their view the main tasks before Indian Communists now were the following:—

(1) To regard the Indian struggle mainly in the light of a colonial national liberation struggle against foreign imperailism and native feudalism, and the treacherous big-bourgeois collaborators who had joined hands with imperialism, and to revise their tactics entirely in that light;

(2) To forge a united-front with all classes, parties, groups and organisation against imperialists and their collaborators.

(3) To distinguish the 'national bourgeoisie' who were opposed to imperialism from the collaborationist big-bourgeoisie, and to treat them as an ally and bring them inside the united front.

(4) To expose the colonising plans of the ithperialsts and

71

their collaborators politically, and again to unite with everybody who are willing to defend the national independence and freedom of India.

These were the immediate tasks which had to be carried out first. It is evident that in the opinion of the Cominform Editorial Board the necessary internal conditions for the commencement of the armed form of struggle or the formation of People's Liberation Armies would not be fulfilled till these initial tasks were carried out. Aimed struggle was certainly a decisive condition for the victory of the national liberation struggles. But the internal political conditions and the correlation of forces in this country had not as yet advanced to that point of maturity so as to enable the movement to take the character of an armed struggle ('general uprising', 'wielding of arms', the 'Telengana way' etc. in terms of the Ranadivite Pout-Bureau) or "to allow" the formation of Liberation Armies.

No basic change

These are in short the salient points of the directive of the Cominform Editorial. So far its basic political content or its emphasis on the national liberationist democratic character of the present phase of mass-struggle in India was concerned, it cannot be said however that any basic change ,was involved in the Cominform directive from the general stand-point of the Calcutta Thesis of the CPI, or from that ofthe inaugural address ofZhdanov to the Cominform Conference in September, 1947. The essential political content ofthe programme of Democratic Front as outlined by the Second Congress of the CPI in 1948, as well as that of the Zhdanov speech was principally based, like the new Cominforni directive, on the strategy of a democratic anti-imperialist national liberation struggle against Anglo-American imperialism, and not on that of Socialist revolution or on class and mass actions under the leadership of the proletariat for the overthrow of capitalism. The main enemy was Anglo-American imperialism and not the imperialist capitalist system as such or the bourgeois order of the society.

Zhdanov Thesis reiterated

Zhdanov had made it unmistakably clear in his inaugural Cominform speech in 1947 that even in highly advanced capitalist and metropolitan countries like Great Britain, France, and Italy- resistance to imperialism (esp. America) for the defence of national independence and sovereignty were to be the main political planks of the mnovement to be organised and led by the Communists. The Communist Parties of these countries were therefore directed by Zhdanov—

To unite their efforts on the basis of a common anti-imperialist and democratic platform, and to gather around them all the democratic and patriotic forces of the people.

He further said—

Communists must support, all the really patriotic elements who do not want their countries to be imposed upon, who want to resist enthralment to foreign capital and to uphold their national sovereignty. The Communists must be the leaders in enlisting all anti- fascist and freedom loving elements in the struggle against the new American expansionist plans for enslavement of Europe. (mc International Situation pp. 46-47)

'Democracy' and 'National Liberation' Only

National honour, independence, lasting peace and popular democracy-these were to be the main slogans of the day and communists everywhere (and those of France. Italy and Great Britain in particular) were enjoined to "act as courageous sentinels of *enduring peace, popular democracy, of the national sovereignty, liberty and independence* of their countries." and "to take the lead of all the forces prepared to uphold *national honour and independence."* [3]

No Socialist Revolution

There was no reference to Socialist revolution, class struggle or overthrow of capitalism anywhere in this lengthy peroration of the CPSU spokesman before the Comminform, except a passing one to the possibility of "*paving* the way for entry on to the *path of* Socialist development," in the case of the new democratic states of Eastern Europe where the process of popular democratic revolution was more or less complete. There is hardly any scope of misunderstanding here. The appropriate time for preparing the ground for a transition to socialism will come only after the establishment of popular democracy, so that the immediate historic objective of the entire world movement from West Europe to East Asia would remain confined for the present, within the political limits and class alliances of a national democratic struggle against American or Anglo-American imperialism.

The Cominform Editorial only reiterated the same thing with reference to India-with particular emphasis on the necessity of drawing upon and closely following the experiences of the Chinese Liberation movement as led by the CP. China.

Notes:

1. Liu Shao Chi is one of the most important members of the Polit-Bureau of the Chinese CP and is regarded as the most important theoretician of the party after Mao Tse-Tung himself and the ablest exponent of Mao Tse-Ttmg's theory of People's Democracy. The entire Cominform Editorial article echoes Liu Shao-Chi's views and its operative parts which we quoted above are literal word for word repetitions of certain portions of the summary he gave in his speech to the TUCAA, of experiences of the Chinese liberation movement and of the conditions of victory.

2. Liu Shao Chi's remarks in this connection are rather significant. When speaking of armed struggles he also mentioned these countries only, excluding India specifically and said that-"the fighters of national liberation wars in Viet Nam, Burma, Indonesia, Malaya and Philippines are acting entirely correctly." But he kept absolutely mum about "armed liberation struggles" and "uprisings" organised by the CPI He also emphasised the imperative necessity of forming People's Liberation Armies "whenever and wherever possible." It is evident that armed struggle must not have, in his view, seemed possible in India at the present stage of the movement. The

implications are clear : any attempt that might have been made in India to give the movement the character of armed uprising and seizure-of-power struggles must have been entirely incorrect.

3. These were the concluding tines of Zhdanov's speech as the Delegate and spokesman of the Communist Party of the Soviet Union to the Cominform Conference containing the formulation of "the special historical task" that devolves upon the Communists of West Europe in the context of the "new post-war alignment of political forces of the formation of the two camps; the impnialist anti-democratic camp led by USA and Great Britain, and the anti-imperialist and democratic camp led by the USSR and based on the USSR and the People's Democracies.' The Cominform declaration reproduced these passages of the CPSU Delegate's address literally, which thus became the fundamental Thesis and Platform of Action for the entire Cominferm and for the Stalinist Communists through- out the world (See: Report of the Frist Cominform Conference; Warsaw, September 1947; and the Decimation of the, Communist Information Bureau as published in "Lasting Peace" No. I. 1947).

Genesis of Left Deviation

Basic 'reformism' of Ranadive line

It is evident that as an application of the Zhdanov thesis in the concrete national political situation of India after the Mountbatten Award and the so-called 'transfer of power' the Ranadive Thesis could not certainly transcend the basic limitations set on it by the political formulations of the former, which guides and determines the entire political outlook of the Cominform and the Stalinist world movement. In spite of outward left embellishments its general standpoint was elaborated within the theoretical frame-work of the same nationalist-oppositional, democratic social-reformist political outlook as the former, and was as much removed from the immediate historic perspective of a proletarian Socialist revolution and from the point of view of proletarian class-struggle against Capitalism. From this fundamental standpoint there could, therefore, be no fundamental difference between the Calcutta Thesis of the CPI and the new Cominform directive. But demands of partisan political expediency made the new 'left' leadership which came to power in the party in 1948 very much concerned about keeping the national-democratic reformist content of their professed leftism as much concealed from the eyes of the rank-and-file by stretching the scope of the theoretical formulations of Zhdanov to the maximum extent possible and without coming into a too obvious or direct contradiction with them. Political terminology was therefore often deliberately employed in a equivocal sense, giving an outward significance opposite to what was really intended, reformist qualification were kept cleverly hidden here and there behind a maze of left trappings, and would be often surreptitiously smuggled in behind a spate of revolutionary phrase-mongering. Demonstrative references were made to Socialist revolution and the tasks of Socialist construction in order to create the impression that the people's Democratic Revolution was really nothing but a process of completing the unfinished task of bourgeois democratic revolution under a proletarian leadership and would immediately go forward to the overthrow of capitalism and to socialist revolution. But in spite of everything the basic political formulations of the Ranadive Thesis about the anti-imperialist and national democratic character of the Indian revolution, even after the Mountbatten Plan and 'transfer of power' to the hands of the Indian bourgeoisie, and the principal strategic tasks that faced the party in that background, were couched in almost identical terms as the Cominform Editorial article.

The nationalist reformist context of these formulations can easily be sifted out from amidst the jungle of seemingly left phraseology with but little difficulty. The Cominform Editorial, as we have seen, especially sought to emphasise the democratic anti-imperialist, colonial national-liberationist character of the Indian mass-struggle. Outward left trappings notwithstanding, the Calcutta Thesis also did the same. Some excerpts from the Calcutta Thesis on these topics may be quoted here relevantly.

Ranadive Thesis On Mountbatten Award

This is what the Calcutta Thesis said about the the Mountbatten Award.

.....The Mountbatten Plan partitioned India...It is one of the biggest attacks on the unity and integrity of the democratic movement.

...The plan keeps the princes, the age-old friends of the imperialist order, intact.

...The leading economic strings are still in the hands of the imperailists, who successfully use them to make the bourgeosie move against the masses, crush democratic revolution and establ ished a new line up of imperialism, princes, landlords and the bourgeoisie.

....The Mountbatten Plan is the expression of the alliance against the democratic revolution,... What the Mountbatten Plan has given to the people is not real but fake independence... Britain's domination has not ended, but the form of domination has changed....the bourgeoisie is granted a share of state power (subservient to imperialism) in order to disrupt and drown the national democratic revolution.... (pp38-40)

On Nehru Government and 'Big' business

Then follows its views about Nehru Government, the Thesis said:

It (the Nehru Govt.) has not solved, said the Thesis, a single problem of the democratic revolution... Indian Big-business and the Government are mortgaging Indian economy to Anglo-American capital in their selfish interests. The natural result of this is not only economic but indirect political domination, so that both[1] the economy and the political freedom are being mortgaged to the Anglo-American imperialists (pp 45-46).

The reference to "Big Business" here, and repeated in pp, 23, 24, 26, 27, 42, 45 and 48, make it amply clear that by referring to the Indian bourgeoisie as having gone "collaborationist' (in its relations, vis-a-vis imperialism) it is precisely 'big' business and 'big' bourgeoisie which the CPI leadership had in mind. Although by repeating the term 'capitalist' and bourgeoisie without the qualifying adjective 'big' a little bit too often, it deliberately sought to create the misleading impression that henceforward they would move against the Indian bourgeoisie as a whole and rally mass forces for fighting the entire class on lines of proletarian class-struggle. As a matter of fact by putting the term "Big Business" in parenthesis immediately after the term "Indian bourgeoisie" at the outset in p 23, it was ensured that the terms were to be taken interchangeably. In p 42, it was clearly said that the Congress Government "was carrying the plans of big business."

79

One of the main charges about Ranadive's left-deviation relate to his characterisation of the entire Indian bourgeoisie as collaborators of imperialism which, it is alleged, prevented the party from attracting "fellow travellers" from other sections of the bourgeoisie, who are not so 'big', especially the middle bourgeoisie and small capitalists etc., to the cause of its 'national liberation struggle. The statements of Mao Tse-Tung, Liu Shao Chi, Li LI San and other Chinese leaders point out on the other hand that one Of the main conditions which enabled the Chinese CP to build up its leadership was that it found the correct policy in differentiating the "national bourgeoisie" from the collaborator big bourgeoisie or "compradore bourgeoisie" subservient to foreign imperialism and treating the former as an ally. The line of Ranandive Thesis apparently treats the entire Indian bourgeoisie as an enemy. If we care to read between the lines, however, we would easily understand which section of the bourgeoisie Ranadive had in mind particularly, although he sought to create the opposite sort of impression in the minds of the uninitiated.

Against the Colonial Order

The Calcutta thesis asserted :

The desire for collaboration (between Anglo-American imperialism and the Indian bourgeoisie or Big business) takes the shape of retaining the colonial order...

The collaboration thus represents an economic and political alliance against the democratic revolution through which alone the people can liberate themselves from the yoke of the colonial order, of landlordism, of the princes and foreign and home capitalists. In the background of this correlationship of forces what was to be the character of the coming revolution in the opinion of the authors of the Calcutta Thesis? This is what the thesis said very clearly.

'New' phase of bourgeois democratic revolution

The old phase of the bourgeois democratic revolution is over, a phase in which the bourgeoisie was in the anti-imperialist camp. To-day the entire trend of events demand a democratic state of workers, toiling peasants and the oppressed petty-bourgeoisie as the only rallying slogan to surge forward to the defeat of imperialism and its bourgeois allies and the emancipation of the people (P-74).

It was in other words, a new phase of the bourgeois-democratic revolution (though new, still a bourgeois and democratic revolution all the same, from the point of view of its social content) that was now called for according to the Ranadive Thesis. This new phase was precisely nothing other than the people's Democratic Revolution.

'Simultaneous' building up of Socialism

In order to make it seem that the People's Democratic revolution was really the prelude to the Socialist revolution it was .added here that it "has to be achieved for the completion of the tasks of the democratic revolution and for the simultaneous building up of Socialism." But obviously completion of the tasks of democratic revolution came first, and by employing the phrase 'building up of Socialism,' instead of Socialist revolution in this connection, a deliberate attempt was made to confuse basic issues and confound the rank-and-file into thinking that People's Democratic Revolution was really indistinguishable from Socialist Revolution. In case of difficulty it would be possible to explain matters in terms of Zhdanov's reference to 'paving the way for entry to the path of Socialist development' in East European People's Democratic states.

The 'Democratic' Front

It was on this theoretical premise that the CPI programme of the Democratic Front was formulated. A glance even at the first few lines of this programme would be sufficient to convince anybody that the fundamental political outlook of the new leaders of the CPI, Ranadive and his colleagues, who were responsible for the 1948 Calcutta Thesis, definitely moved within the limits of an anti-imperialist, bourgeois-democratic, national movement and did not overstep those limits by a jot. The apparent left-orientation of the new CPI political line of 1948 compared to the Joshi line of collaboration with imperialism and the national bourgeoisie, the heroic invectives that were hurled against the Nehru Government and capitalists, need not therefore be taken in their face value or regarded as a 'left-deviation' in the basic formulation of the character of the coming phase of Indian revolution in terms of a Socialist transformation of the existing capitalist-cum-imperialist-feudal, semi-colonial social order. That was initially ruled out by the pre-determined ideological moorings of the Calcutta Thesis based on the national-liberationist, popular democratic outlook laid down by Zhdanov and the Cominform for the entire Stalinist world movement outside Soviet Union.

Alleged post-Calcutta deviations

This statement might seem rather strange in view of the universal chorus of indictment that has been raised in Stalinist circles lately against Ranadive's left-deviations since the publication of the Cominform Edito . We have already seen that it has been openly alleged, and subsequently meekly admitted by Ranadive and his Polit-Bureau colleagues also, that they had denied the colonial status of India under the domination of British imperialism after the grant of the so-called 'independence' and 'transfer of power,' they had identified India with a fully-developed bourgeois capitalist state under domination of the Indian bourgeoisie, and that they underestimated or even totally neglected the prime historic necessity of waging struggle against imperialism-feudalism, against the colonial domination of India by British monopoly-capital and the native princes and other feudal elements who together with a subservient group of native big bourgeoisie rule the Country today. Ranadive leadership was consequently led — it is further alleged — to revise the Zhdanov definition of People's Democratic Revolution as applied to colonial countries and the primarily national democratic character of that revolution. It had rather identified it directly with the phase of proletarian Socialist revolution for the overthrow of capitalism. The objection of Ranadive's critics are directed — it should be noted not so much against the Calcutta Thesis itself — which in spite of its recently discovered 'incorrect' 'left-deviationist' formulations — were unhesitatingly accepted two years ago by the entire Party Congress including many of Ranadive's bitterest critics of to-day. Their indicments are especially directed against the subsequent documents of the Polit-Bureau which sought to give an authoritative interpretation of the main political line adopted at Calcutta viz: the PB. Resolutions on People's Democracy and the Agrarian question (December 1948; published in Communist No. 1, 1949), and the Report on Strategy and Tactics, which contained a vehement criticism of certain aspects of Mao Tse-Tung' line of policy in China and the Mao version of People's Democracy.

More apparent than real

Without entering into the details of these charges here, it can be safely asserted, in view of the quotations from crucial passages of the Calcutta Thesis given above (which provide in a sense the theoretical premise for the entire Democratic Front Programme), that the alleged left-deviations of the Ranadive line, as represented by that thesis and its subsequent elaborations, or its contradictions with the basic nationalist-oppositional, democratic and social reformist point of view of international Stalinism and the Cominform, are more apparent than real. The subsequent theoretical elaborations of the Calcutta Thesis must be read and interpreted in the context of the basic outlook represented by that thesis, unless it was openly repudiated by Ranadive; which he never did. Whatever contradictions there were arose, as already indicated above, from the clumsy endeavours of the CPI leadership to conceal the essentially reformist class-collaborationist character of the Stalinist theory of People's Democracy, and to pass it off as a variety of near-Socialism. These self-contradictions were already inherent in the formulations of Calcutta Thesis. Subsequently however under the impact of internal struggle for power amongst the leaders of the Party, and the unavoidable necessity of whipping up and mobilising petty-bourgeois leftism of the youthful rank-and-file of the party for launching 'militant mass-actions' against the Congress Government these contradictions became increasingly glaring. These naturally gave rise to all sorts of theoretical muddle-headedness, self deceptive confusions of thought and a wobbly leftism, which was not always much to the liking of the so-called 'left' leaders themselves.

Demands of petty-bourgeois leftism

In order to hurriedly get some sort of show of mass-opposition and organise resistance against the anti-Soviet and pro Anglo-American foreign policy of the Nehru Government pursuant to the over-all plan for resistance to "aggressive Anglo-American imperialist plans within the limits of the power-rivalries between USA, Great-Britain and the Soviet Union, as laid down by Zhdanov at the Cominform Conference, the CPI leadership had to fall back in the absence of any active or broad based political-support for its policies amongst the masses, on its own party-organisation and its severely depleted rank of militant activists. The reformist bourgeois and petty-bourgeois 'lib-lab's who had swelled the ranks of the party during the "People's War" days made hurried exit as soon as there was any talk of struggle against the government of the day. The following of the party amongst the working class and the peasantry were never very widespread, except in a very few isolated localities, and in most places party cadres were composed mainly of young enthusiasts coming from the petty-bourgeoisie and radical intelligentsia.1 In order to throw the predominantly petty-bourgeois cadres of the party into the fray willy-nilly and earn praises from Soviet spokesmen like Balabushevich, he had to indoctrinate them with favourite left-revolutionist catch-phrases of that class, to inspire them with the stirring thought that they were going to overthrow native capitalists like the Tatas and Birlas, Anglo-American imperialists, the Native Princes, landlords and all feudal riff-raff at a single stroke, and unleash by their 'militant actions' a mighty revolutionary upsurge of the toiling masses under the leadership of their party for the establishment of Socialism. Compelled by the logic of their international policy to launch some sort of struggle and create some sort of trouble for the Nehru Government, so as to prove to the outside world that the Congress allies of Anglo-America had entirely failed to stabilise the political situation in India on their behalf, or to appease the insurgent mass-forces (led by the Communists!) CPI leadership could not avoid catering to the demands of infantile petty-bourgeois leftism and cheap revolution-mongering both ideologically and tactically.

Petty-Bourgeois 'leftism' foisted on People's Democratic Reformism

Ideologically Ranadive could hope to inspire the youthful petty bourgeois cadres of the party only by imparting a dazzling left — the anti-capitalist veneer on people's democratic reformism; tactically by glorifying their adventurist-terroristic hurrah-actions, divorced from any contact with the masses or their consciousness — as "the most advanced and revolutionary form of struggle", and creating the illusion that the masses could by these means be brought "to the point at which they will echo the party's cry of ending the government." It had therefore to be constantly dinned into their ears that the situation is "full of revolutionary possibilities" and the masses could be induced step by step, to move forward to "general strikes, political strikes and general uprising." The rank-and-file must not be

85

allowed to get discouraged by the fact that neither the masses in general, nor the working class, were responding to their hurrah-tactics. They must be constantly administered self-deceptive pep-talks about "uneven development of the consciousness of the masses" and about the surety of most elementary struggles "setting in motion forces for a general uprising" in the objective background of a rapidly unfolding "revolutionary period." It was precisely these two aspects of Ranadive's alleged 'leftism,' demanded by the immediate practical exigencies of demonstrative political actions against the Congress Government which the CPI was called upon to organise in the name of "resistance to the aggressive plans of Anglo-American Imperialism," that found expression in the Polit-Bureau Resolutions on "People's Democracy" and the "Agrarian Question" and his Report on "Strategy and Tactics."

Ranadive's Theoretical quandaries

His attempt to give a Socialist and near-Socialist 'left' twist to People's Democracy by stretching the scope of its possible scientific political definition to the utmost, involved him in the queerest theoretical and ideological contradictions. These attempts often made him liable to formal charges of 'left-deviation.' For he was often compelled to keep the basic class-collaborationist reformist aspects of People's Democracy deliberately concealed from the view of his 'militant' rank-and-file' by 'leftist' glosses. But at the sametime, essentially moving withing the basic ideological frame-work of Stalinism, he was never able — nor did he actually want—to cut himself adrift from the reformist nationalist-oppositional moorings of 'popular democracy' altogether. Precariously depending on Zhdanov's guarded definition about the possible course of the next phase of development of People's Democratic States of Eastern Europe in terms of preparing the pre-conditions for undertaking the tasks of Socialist Construction ("*paving the way for entry* on to the path of"...etc., —'International Situation', pp 9-10) and the Calcutta Congress formulation of its tasks of People's

Democratic Revolution as the "completion of the tasks of democratic revolution and the *simultaneous* building up of Socialism," he proceeded within the PB Resolution on People's Democracy to make a hotch-potch of everything. He termed the coming People's Democratic Revolution in India as a potpourri 'mixture' of the February and October Revolutions, "an interlacing of democratic and socialist Revolutions", for the establishment of "a democratic dictatorship of the proletariat and peasantry which quickly passes into the Dictatorship of the Proletariat." He apparently wanted to eliminate the bourgeoisie from any share in the participation in this revolution, or in the new state-power that would emerge in course of the People's Democratic Revolution. But at once got a theoretic funk and interpreted it as only meaning "*eliminating the political* rule of the bourgeoisie" for the present, and subsequently going over to policy of "squeezing out capitalist elements in the countryside" after the new state comes into being. He warned the party at the same time, against prematurely raising the slogan of the Dictatorship of the Proletariat so as not to alienate "the intermediary strata, parties and classes," for a large section of petty-bourgeoisie and middle peasants were coming into conflict with the bourgeoisie. By raising the slogan of proletarian dictatorship the "democratic front" would get disrupted and play into the hands of the bourgeoisie. In order to disguise his own colossal confusion of thinking, he made a play with the idea of the "hegemony of the proletariat" over the "bloc of peasantry, petty-bourgeoisie people etc.,"—a bloc in which the bourgeoisie would have no place and which will "go beyond bourgeois democracy" through nationalisation of industries etc. towards Socialism and proletarian dictatorship, and so on and so forth. But he could never bring himself to raise the issue of a proletarian Socialist Revolution in a direct and straight-forward manner as the immediate historic objective for the party after the installation of the bourgeoisie to the posiiton of the direct ruling class in place of imperialism and native feudalism, which had withdraw from the forefront and taken shelter behind the national bourgeoisie and their ruling power. He knew that he was prevented from doing that by the basic formulation of the Zhdanov thesis to which he had to swear allegiance always as a loyal Stalinist.

Lenin's 'Two Tactics' turned upside down

The depth of the theoretical quandary in which he landed himself in this way ultimately led him to make on entire topsy-turvy of Lenin's celebrated formulation of the 'Two Tactics' about the tasks and class alignments of the bourgeois-democratic and Socialist revolutions and confuse one with the other. He urged the proletariat and the CPI in all seriousness to complete the tasks of democratic revolution with the forces and class-alignments of a Socialist Revolution.[2]

Ranadive's theoretical performance is only paralleled, it should be remarked here, by the opposite sort of theoretical travesty perpetrated by the latest East-European exponents of People's Democracy like Dimitrov, Beirut and Hilary Mine, who seem to think that it is possible (and in East-Europe it 'has actually' been possible!) to successfully accomplish a Socialist revolution and to carry out the functions of the Dictatorship of the Proletariat with the class alignments of a democratic revolution, without any violence or civil war, "thanks to the all-round help liberally rendered by the Soviet Union" (see: Reports by Dimitrov & Beirut to the Workers Parties of Bulgaria & Poland; Lasting Peace No. 1, 1949.)

It is queer that since the publication of the Cominform Editorial it is being indignantly charged on all hands in Indian Stalinist circles that Ranadive had the 'impertinence' or 'cheek' to revise Zhdanov's definition of People's Democracy; but nobody seems to care or to have even noticed that he had the fool-hardiness to revise the classic formulations of Lenin himself! Perhaps Zhdanov is now theoretically more important to them than Lenin— after all Lenin could never envisage the "new type of state" that People's Democracy represents, and which was theoretically and practically analysed by the great

Zhdanov especially for our epoch!

Leftism tolerated despite self-contradictions

The apparent left-orientation imparted to the theory of People's Democracy by Ranadive, and its inevitable contradictions with the essential nationalist-oppositional democratic-reformist content of that theory as envisaged by the international Stalinist leadership, seemed to cause no harm so long as it helped the CPI to rally the forces of petty-bourgeois leftism in its ranks and hurl them against the bourgeois Congress Government suspected of slavishly toeing the anti-Soviet foreign policy line of Anglo-America. It was for that reason that, in spite of blatant theoretical self-contradictions of the Ranadive formulations from the very beginning, the international leadership went on shouting buck-ups to the CPI, and remained satisfied with veiled hints thrown in now and then, about exploring the chances of possible alliances with bourgeois, middle-bourgeois and petty-bourgeois groups and parties who might be opposed to the dominant big bourgeois or big-business groups having a upper hand in the government at present. All leading Soviet experts on India Zhukov, Alexyev, Dyakov and Balabushevich who discussed the Indian situation in Soviet press from time to time during the last two years since the Calcutta Congress of CPI did the same. But they never ceased patting CPI leadership on the back for their heroic success in organising and leading "the struggle for the hegemony of the working-class" in the "national liberation movement" and building up a broad-based mass resistance to the Congress government's policy of open collaboration with Anglo-America and upholding the cause of the Soviet-led Democratic Camp in this country.[3]

Notes

1. Ranadive's revelations in this respect are interesting. "One of the legacies of the reformist period,' he wrote in his "Report on Strategy & Tactics," is the over-whelmingly petty-bourgeois composition of the Party...The Party was based on the

wrong classes. The working class, the poor and the agricultural workers were neglected... In the name of non-sectarianism, bourgeois and petty bourgeois intellectuals were encouraged with all their faults....

"With Marxist education discouraged.. and with workers not supposed to study Marxism:— it was next to impossible to inspire the workers to join in large numbers" (Communist, No. 4, 1949 p 35-35).

Even the petty-bourgeois elements, he further complained, "were prevented from taking a firm stand against capitalists and reformists and were denounced as 'terrorists,' when their anti-imperialist instincts (!) drove them to take a correct stand"! Naturally in this highly unsatisfactory state of the class-composition of the party which he inherited Ranadive had no other alternative but to rely on these petty-bourgeois militants and their anti-imperialist and their anti-capitalist 'instincts' (whatever that might mean) for the 'struggles' he was required to launch. It should also be remarked here that curiously enough his principal adversary Mr. P. C. Joshi also agrees with these views of Ranadive about the state of party organisation and its membership, with this difference that he refers to conditions to which the party 'degenerated' since his forced exit from leadership! In his letter to Foreign Comrades he reports that "regular contact with the masses is broken. Small squads of student comrades in their teens, guided by a fanatical underground worker, with sometimes a lad or two from the working class thrown in, are sent out when a strike call is given or a meeting is possible." And further, he says in another place "the working class is not responding to our practical lead." He also complains about the lack of Marxist education in the ranks (Views, No. 1. p 28-29); but magnanimously admits his own share of responsibility for it.

2. The actual formulation of famous 'Two Tactics' of Lenin runs as follows : 'Democratic Revolution' :

"The Proletariat must carry to completion the democratic revolution, by allying itself to the mass of peasantry in order to crush by force the resistance of autocracy and paralyse the instability of the bourgeoisie".

The appropriate slogan for this stage of the revolution according to Lenin is the "Democratic Dictatorship of the Proletariat and the Peasantry". Socialist Revolution : "The Proletariat must accomplish the Socialist revolution by allying to itself the mass of semi-proletarian elements of the population in order to crush by force the resistance of the bourgeoisie and to paralyse the stability of the peasantry and petty-bourgeoisie".

The appropriate slogan for this stage of the revolution is the "Dictatorship of the Proletariat".

Ranadive amended Lenin's formulation in the following manner: "The proletariat must accomplish the people's democratic revolution by allying itself to the agricultural workers and poor peasants-followed by the middle peasants-in order to isolate the bourgeoisie and crush their resistance by force" ("Strategy & Tactics', Communist No. 4, P. 42). But the slogan of Socialist revolution or the Dictatorship of the proletariat must not be raised "because intermediary stratas, parties and classes have not yet exhausted their possibilities and therefore, a bloc with them cannot be ruled out" ('On People's Democracy'). What then is the appropriate slogan for this stage? According to Ranadive, it is Democratic Dictatorship of the Proletariat and the Peasantry (together with intermediary sarata, parties and classes). But Democratic Dictatorship is the culmination of bourgeois democratic revolution and demands on entirely different line of tactics than that outlined by Ranadive. The class alignment and the tasks of the People's Democratic Revolution as described by Ranadive belong neither lo Democratic Revolution nor Socialist revolution completely, and muddle the basic issues hopelessly.

3. As V. V. Balabushevich pointed out, the following were the principal achievements of the CPI during this period from the point of view of international Stalinism : (I) "resolutely exposing bourgeois machinations directed towards keeping India tied to the Anglo-American bloc" ....(2) The CPI has noted that "the South East Asia block and the Pacific Pact are instruments for the struggle against the rising national liberation movement in the countries of S.E. Asia and preparation in the East for a base of an attack against the USSR;" and last but by no means the least, (3) the CPI "emphasises that working masses of India look upon the Soviet Union as the leading force in the struggle against world reaction". These were certainly imposing achievements and the tactics of CPI, whatever might be their lapses here and there in matters of theory — lapses dictated by the necessity of organising militant mass-actions against Anglo-American imperialism and their Indian bourgeois (or big-bourgeois) stooges — served their purpose all right.

Logic of Self-Contradiction

Ranadive comes up against Mao

Encouraged by these encomiums and also carried over by the logic of the basically opportunist left-theoretic craze which infected the party from top to bottom about this time (Dec 1948 July August 1949) Ranadive moved step by step into a position which might some day come in manifest contradiction with the practical exigencies of the basic world-policy of international Stalinism and Soviet power-politics which had originally called for the initial left-turn in September 1947.

Under the circumstances of 1947-48 the demonstrative swing to the left was dictated to a great extent by practical necessities of rehabilitating the party in the confidence of the masses after the ignominious betrayals of the People's War Phase. It also became increasingly necessary, as we have seen, for enthusing the romantic leftism and millitancy of youthful petty-biourgeois cadres of the party and throw them at the head of 'mass-actions' to be launched against the Nehru Government. But driven by the logic of inherent self-contradiction of a basically reformist political strategy trying to wear a' left' mask and carry out certain adventurist' left' tactical manoeuvres for securing its own limited reformist objectives, the CPI leadership brought themselves to a dangerous theoretical and tactical ground which came into open contradiction with the fundamental postulates of Stalinist reformism. On the agrarian question, for example, in the background of the Congress Government's demagogic propaganda about the new legislative measures for the abolition of landlordism with compensation, it was supposed that in order to out-manoeuvre the Congress and to broad-base the party amongst the peasant masses especially amongst poor peasantry and the agricultural workers, the agrarian policy of the party might with advantage be recast in terms of 'class struggle' between the rural bourgeoisie and rural proletariat, between the rich peasantry or 'Kulaks' and the poor peasantry and agricultural workers. This would also enable the party to appear theoretically 'more left' than anybody else. Prompted by these motives the slogans of 'land-nationalisation' and 'redistribution of land' in favour of poor peasantry and landless agriculturists were eventually put forward boldly (PB Resolution— On the Agarian question, Dec. 1948-Jan. 1949) and nonchalantly, while veteran leaders of East-European People's Democracies including late Dimitrov even, hesitated to speak of land-nationalisaton and considered it having "no practical significance"for their countries (see LPPD No 1, 1949 —Report to the CC.Plenum of the Bulgarian Workers Party)! Last but not the least, as a measure of self-defence in the partisan struggle for leadership within the party, against Joshi-ites and their allies, who wanted to take their stand on the comparatively moderate class-collaborationist formulations of People's Democracy put forward by Mao Tse-Tung in China, Ranadive also 'dared' come out with an open and vehement criticism of the reformism of Mao Tse-Tung and certain aspects of his theory and practice of People's Democracy in China which provided the ground work of the entire popular democratic outlook for Stalinism.[1] He might have been encouraged in making this criticism by putting credit in speculations given currency by Anglo-American imperialist press about this time about Mao Tse-Tung turning out to be rebel like Tito eventually. He therefore sought to reinforce his own theoretical position vis-a-vis those of his rivals by swearing allegiance to the classics of Marx, Engels, Lenin, Stalin, and contrasting Zhdanov's formulations about People's Democracy with those of the 'revisionist' Tito-Mao.

'Leftism' exhausts utility

Here evidently Ranadive overshot his mark. For by the time Ranadive remembered his Marxism, the civil war in china was drawing to a close with the defeat and rout of the America backed KMT-Chiang clique and the People's Republic of China

94

was proclaimed.Mao Tse-Tung and the Chinese CP. as well as the People's Republic of China with its specific economic, social and political policies based on collaboration between labour and capital and liberal agrarian reforms, were already far more powerful and tremendously important factors in moulding the world policies of Stalinism, and in the *real-politik* of Soviet power-rivalry vis-avis Anglo-America, than Ranadive could imagine in the excitement and fury of his underground partisan struggles for leadership against Joshiites, pro-joshiites and other political rivals. His theoretic left aberrations might in other circumstances have been ignored altogether or he might have been allowed sufficient time to retrace his steps and withdraw himself gradually from the precarious position to which he had been compelled unwillingly to betake himself. He seemed to have realised the enormity of his own indiscretions and tried to make humble amends at the earliest opportunity, as his lengthy telegram of congratulation to Mao, on the latter's election as the President of the People's Republic of China, amply testify.

A new turn in international alignment

But the emergence of the People's Republic of China and its tremendous significance as a new decisive factor in world politics altered the correlationship offerees in the international arena in such a way that compelled every power with some interest or stake in the Far East including the Government of India also, to reassess its own position and recast its policies accordingly. The intensification of Anglo-American inter-imperialist contradictions all'over the world, and in the Pacific and South East-Asian regions in particular, by this time, inevitably caused an open divergence in Anglo-American policies in the Far East. In consideration of its trading interests and other financial stakes in China, Britain was impelled to accord formal diplomatic recognition to the communist-led People's Republic of China in the face of decided American opposition, closely followed by India and other Commonwealth countries.[2] The rift in the Anglo-American imperailist camp was widening. In opposition to American endeavours to prop up and politically reinforce its unchallenged naval and military sway over the Pacific by imposing puppet regimes in Korea, Japan, Philippines, Formosa and Indo China, and thursting prongs at the sametime, towards South East Asia— an exclusively British sphere of influence till recently, Britain tried to throw up its own defence-line by rallying together the support of Commonwealth powers. Both USA and Britain were faced with the challenge of sweeping upsurge of the revolutionary freedom movements of peoples of these regions. In the background of its own conflict of interests with the United States, British imperialism found it more advisable to combine a policy of brutal repression against liberation movements in its own domains like Malaya, with an understanding with the new governments that have actually come to power on the crest of popular upsurge, provided these governments agreed to play satellite role of colonial capitalist states, or at-least agree to accord reciprocal recognition to British finacial interests and refrain from making too drastic in-roads on the rights of trade and property of British nationals in the manner of assurance already given by popular democratic People's Republic of China.

Nehru Government reassesses its own position

The Nehru Government in India is faithfully following the foot-step of Britain in this respect uptil now. But it is also trying at the same time to find its own bearings independently— so far as it lies in its power—to reach to a possible line of modus vivendi by coming to terms with the new forces that were raising heads in neighbouring countries and save themselves from the sweeping catastrophe of war and revolution which threaten to envelop the capitalist world as a whole sooner or later. The Nehru Government has also been compelled in other words, to reassess its own position in the light of the altered correlationship of international forces since the emergence of the Chinese People's Republic and has correspondingly induced others to recast their evaluations about itself.

1948 line needs overhaul

The last six months of 1949 has in effect set in motion forces in the international arena which makes earlier policy formulations of two years back entirely out of date, and indications are not wanting which go to show that international Stalinist movement has, in the background of the shifts that have inevitably occurred in world scene in recent past, felt the necessity of recasting its line and tactics with regard to India.

The CPSU also

We have to bear this fact in mind particularly when we sit to consider the impending changes in the political line of the Communist party of India. This change has not come, we must remember firstly, because of any conscious revolt on the part of the leading party-cadres outside Polit-Bureau or conscious Marxist-Leninist elements of the rank-and-file against the alleged anti-Marxist, anti-Lenin-Stalin opportunist left deviations of Ranadive andvPolit-Bureau. The initiative or the signal for this change came from the above on behalf of the international leadership as represented by the Cominform Editorial Board.

Although the Cominform directives has in effect asked the CPI to overhaul its strategy and tactics completely and follow the China-way, it has to be noted that even the message of Mao Tse-Tung in his reply to Ranadive's congratulatory telegram that the Indian people must follow the China-way did not induce the Party-whether leadership or rank-and-file—to change or amend their line. It should also be remembered that the theoretic 'left-sectarian' and other 'deviations' which are now being discovered in the Ranadive line were perpetrated more than two years or at least one and half years back. But nobody whether Cominform leaderhship or the 'now-wise' leaders who are tearing the Ranadive line to pieces seemed to care that there were any deviations or contradictions at all. Nothing changes the Stalinist pattern of thought as we have seen earlier, without the cue of that change coming from the international centre of the Stalinist world-movement—the CPSU and Cominform etc. It will therefore be necessary to keep our eyes open to that aspect of the question as well, to the necessity that might have been felt by the leadership of the CPSU in the background of recent developments in Asia and the East, of changing its asessments about the situation in India. That will serve to explain both the Cominform directive to the CPI and the tirade against Ranadive's 'left' deviations.

Notes:

1. Ranadive's revelations in this respect are interesting. "One of the legacies of the reformist period,' he wrote in his "Report on Although Mao Tse Tung's theory was originally propounded in 1940 and has held ground ever since in the international Stalinist movement including the CPI. Ranadive suddenly remembered his Marxism after 8 years, and pronounced Mao's sympathies for the development of Capitalism in China to be "reactionary" and "in contradiction to world understanding of the Communist Parties" (On Strategy and Tactics'; Communist No 4. 1949; PP-77-80) The CPI Polit-Bureau and the reconstituted Central Committee has since unconditionally withdrawn this criticism and apologised to MaoTse-Tung and Chinese Communist Party for it.

2. In point of time India's recognition of the PRC was announced earlier than that of Britain.

The Stalinist World Out-Look

Meaning of the 'Shift' in terms of international strategy

It is well-known that every important change-over in the national political line of the CPI, like that of every other national section of the world Stalinist movement in the past two decades, has always followed up prior changes in the foreign-policy line of the Soviet Union. The international strategy for the whole movement and the major tactical moves of every national Communist Party are derived without exception from the premise of the foreign policy of the Soviet State. The failure to conform to the dictates of this basic line of international strategy, to adjust national policies to the expediency manoeuvres, zig-zags and tactical shifts of that line is invariably liable to be regarded as a deviation, 'right' or 'left', 'reformist-opportunist' or "dogmatic sectarian', according to the specific circumstances of the case. In order to understand the significance of the new shift in the political line of the CPI in the background of Stalinist world strategy and to arrive at a correct appraisal of the actual reasons which prompted the Cominform Centre to intervene in the affairs of the CPI at this particular juncture and enforce this shift we shall have to seek indications of a corresponding change in the CPSU-Cominform international tactical line with regard to India at least. A shift in the national-political line of any Stalinist Party is almost inconceivable without a shift in the international tactical line— especially so in the present case, in the context of the consistent and loud approval for the old (1948-49) line of the CPI till the very close of the last year.

Around the 'Central Axis'

We shall also have to bear in mind in this connection, the fundamental ideological and theoretical premises upon which the International Stalinist Communist movement and the CPSU take their stand to-day and within the rigid framework of

99

which the Stalinist Communist Party of every country has to function. This is not because of any alleged pulling of wires by the Soviet bosses from Moscow[1] seeking to rule the world with the help of a carefully indoctrinated diabolic Fifth Column organisation set up in every country as the die-hard Anglo-American capitalist press would seem to suggest in their fits of Goebbelsque harangues against the USSR. There is no such Moscow directed world conspiracy. But, nevertheless, the fact remains that the entire world Stalinist movement has grown up during the course of the last three decades in an absolute unilateral dependence on ideological and political guidance from the Communist Party of the Soviet Union. Both ideologically and by logical deduction from the political premises which they have become habituated to take for granted without question, Stalinist Communists in every country have come to regard the defence of the Soviet Union and its political interests as the basic mooring or foundation on which the entire world working class movement should rest, as an article of their fundamental creed. As D. Z. Manuilisky, the CPSU spokesman (now Foreign Minister of Soviet Ukrania and Ukranian representative in the UNO), in the Seventh world Congress of the Communist international declared in 1935—"all key problems of this movement (i.e., the world working class movement, in so far as it is led by the Stalinist Communists), all its tactical problems revolve around the central axis—the reinforcement of the U.S.S.R. as the base of world proletarian revolution."[2]

'In the interests of the people'

The political implications of Manuilisky's statement is clear beyond any scope of misunderstanding. As the foreign policy of the Soviet State (like that of any other state) is inevitably bound up with its international political reinforcement and national defence, logically therefore, all "key problems' of the Stalinist Communist Parties in every country of the world have in practical effect come to revolve round the

100

'axis' of Soviet foreign policy. "The line of foreign policy represented and upheld by the Soviet Union", "writes the woman Soviet publicist N. Sergeyeva in a recent issue of the Moscow weekly New Times. (No. 25, June 1950), "corresponds to the interests of the people and is 'supported" by the masses of all countries." This is a fundamental article of faith with Stalinist Communists all over the world. No matter whether this policy advocates support to the armament programme of M. Laval in pre-war France (1934-35) and calls for uncalled for support to the war-efforts of Anglo-American imperialism in countries like India ('People's War'), whether it leads Stalin and Molotov to enter into Mutual Aid and Non-Aggression pacts with Hitler or sit round the conference table in Yalta and Potsdam with Roosevelt-Truman-Churchill and Attlee for a division of spoils and spheres of influence in Balkans, Middle East and Far East, whether it demands of armed-resistance-forces of working people in France and Belgium to surrender their arms and submit to the rulership of men like De Gaulle and Spaak, whether it directs CP of France to join the French Cabinet and acquiesce in brutal measures of colonial repression in Viet Nam and Madagascar (1946-47)—it always 'corresponds' to the interests of the people and should be supported by the masses!

Departure from Leninism

Granting the theoretical premises of Stalinism there is nothing to be surprised at this. It is the inevitable logical consequence of the abandonment by the leading party of the international working class movement viz: the CPSU of the basic Marxist Leninist standpoint which decides all questions of strategy and tactics from the cardinal point of view of the interests of the international proletarian socialist revolution. Marxism-Leninism judges and decides all questions of political policy in the objective background of the specific alignment of class forces for and against proletarian revolution in each country, and on the world scale, and the concrete historical

101

stage of revolution in a particular country. Marxist-Leninist internationalism inevitably regards the defence of the Soviet Union against all forms of imperialist aggression as one of its sacred tasks. But at the same time it holds fast to Lenin's dictum that "building up the anti-imperialist revolutionary socialist movement in one's own country and rendering all possible help to such movements, and such movements alone, in other countries" is the best form of "internationalism in deeds" and the best form of defence of the USSR that the working class in countries outside Soviet Union can render to-day. It looks upon the Soviet Union "as a link"— the most important link undoutedly—" in the chain of international proletarian revolutions" and always subordinate the specific national state-interests of the USSR at any particular time to permanent interest of international proletarian revolution and not vice versa —that is the central axis round which any problem of strategy and tactics of the entire world working class movement including those of the USSR must revolve in its view if we have to forge ahead to the overthrow of capitalism and the establishment of Socialism and the rule of the working class all over the world. But that no longer represents the point of view or the immediate historic perspective of the CPSU and its leaders.

'For the Defence of SU and Bourgeois Democracy'

It may be remembered here that even one year before Manuilisky elaborated his theory of deciding all key tactical problems of the world working class movement in terms of the defence and reinforcement of the Soviet Union, Stalin himself emphatically disclaimed any intention or responsibility of promoting or rendering any direct or indirect assistance to the revolutionary movements for the overthrow of capitalism in countries outside the frontiers of the Soviet Union to Roy Howard of the American Scripts, Howard news agency (1934). Manuilisky himself had also asserted in the same speech from which we have quoted above that in the background of the rise of Fascism which wanted to unleash a new imperialist war and entertained frankly aggressive intentions against the Soviet Union "the proletariat in most capitalist countries" were not "confronted with the alternative of bourgeois democracy and proletarian democracy" (socialism) and that "bourgeois democracy" (even the so-called democracy of imperialist-capitalist countries like Britain. USA and France) was a "progressive step forward compared with Fascism." In capitalist countries outside the frontiers of USSR — "the base of world proletarian revolution" —the workers were therefore enjoined by Manuilisky, Dimitrov and other Stalinist leaders not only not to fight against capitalism as such, but rather to fight for capitalism in terms of bourgeois democracy, in the name of a struggle against Fascism. It is well-known that it was on this basis that the tactics of 'Popular Front' with anti-Nazi and anti-Fascist capitalist parties, and the world strategy of international 'democratic' people's coalition between USSR, USA and Anglo-French imperialism, were laid down at the Seventh Congress of the Communist International. But for the interlude of the first 21 months of the last war when Soviet Union was practically allied with Nazi Germany against Britain and France in terms of the Mutual Non-aggression Pact (and the various trade and economic agreements which were then negotiated between the two powers) this anti-Fascist Popular Front tactics for the defence of bourgeois democracy dominated the entire political perspective of the Stalinist Communist Parties in every country. We also know how the "imperialist war" suddenly became qualitatively transformed into the "People's War" for the defence of democracy and victory over Fascism on the morrow of the commencement of the Soviet-German War in June 1941 and the formation of the Anglo-US-Soviet Coalition against the Axis. The entire working class movement under the leadership of the Stalinist Communist parties throughout the world was then switched all at once to the support of Anglo-US-Soviet alliance and all opposition against Anglo-American Imperialism were unhesitatingly withdrawn on the plea of anti-Fascist struggle and the defence of democracy. That the motivation behind this 'defence of democracy' actually sprang from the basic line of the defence of the USSR is only too obvious to need any dilation here.

The Leading String

The subsequent development of the course of events and the break up of the People's war coalition after the defeat of Nazi Germany and Japan, has already been indicated above in broad outlines in connection with the turns and twists of the CPI political line since 1945 and the discussion of the post war international line of Stalinism, as formulated by late Andriev Zhdanov in the background of the so-called "Two-camp" divisions of the world. The leading string for Stalinist world strategy and tactics and that of the 'world working class movement' which is under the leadership of Stalinist Communists, has been, furnished at every decisive turn in course of the dizzy developments of the past fifteen years, by " the defence and reinforcement of the USSR." Manuilisky formula holds equally good today as it did on the day when it was first set forth in 1935, with this difference that the slender theoretical reservation about world proletarian revolution which Manuilisky had made at that time in his reference to the SU as its base has been quietly dropped so that only "defence and reinforcement" of the USSR remains as the sole axis of the world movement for Stalinism.

Stalinism today

The two basic theoretic props of the international Stalinist Communist movement to-day are provided by Stalin's theory of 'victory of Socialism and Communism in a single Country' and has parallel theory about the possibility of the peaceful coexistence of the two systems—Socialism and Capitalism side by side for a long period to come' in the present historical epoch. Taken together these two theories have inevitably come to imply the ditching of international

104

proletarian Socialist revolution. There cannot obviously be any prolonged co-existence' for the two systems, Socialism and capitalism, side by side, far less any cooperation (or any possibility of peaceful competition between them) if you go about organising class and mass forces for the overthrow of the latter in countries outside the 'single' socialist country.

'Peaceful Co-existence'

It is not necessary here to enter into any detailed discussion about the different aspects of these two theories and their implications. But the following clearcut reply that Stalin made to Harold E. Stassen (the US Republican Party leader) in his interview with the latter in April 1947, to Stassen's query about his views "whether the two economic systems—socialism and capitalism can exist together in the same modern world in harmony with each other" gives a succinct idea of the Stalinist stand in a general way! "Of course they can," said Stalin, "The differences between them is not of fundamental importance in so far as co-operation is concerned....'

Then further!

"Let us not criticise mutually our systems. Everyone has the -right to follow the system he wants to maintain. Which is better will be said by history...to co-operate one does not need the same systems. One should respect the other system when approved by the people. Only on this basis can we secure co-operation." Stalin reiterated the same view more emphatically in his reply to the open letter of Mr. Henry Wallace and expressed the belief that peaceful settlement of the differences between them "is absolutely necessary in the interests of universal peace". Zhdanov repeated the same idea in almost identical words in his Cominform address. Besides, it should be noted that it is no longer a question of the mere theoretical possibility of the co-existence of the two systems being present there. As Maurice Thorez, the French Communist leader asserted recently at the Plenum of the CP France (June, 1950)—the democratic forces must "enforce the coexistence upon those who reject it.....for the fear that "the victory of the socialist system is inevitable in the peaceful competition between the two systems. "Apparently this means that we must compel the unwilling capitalists to abandon their anti-Soviet imperialist war mongering and live in Peace with Soviet Union. But converse is also true—we must compel the forces fighting against capitalism to make it possible for the latter to "co-exist peacefully with the SU" side by side.

What Lenin had said :

The necessity of strictly adhering to the principle of maintaining entirely non-aggressive and peaceful relations by the Soviet Union as a state, in its code of conduct and international dealings with surrounding states, capitalist or otherwise has thus, however, been transformed by Stalinists in imperceptible degrees into the historical theory of a "prolonged equilibrium between Socialism and Capitalism" and the strategy of class collaboration on the international plane. The imperative historic necessity of organising and preparing for the overthrow of capitalism and proletarian socialist revolution in any country outside the frontiers of the Soviet Union, is totally denied, even in the background of the present epoch of the generalised crisis of imperialism-capitalism which Lenin had termed as the "prelude to international proletarian revolutions." One has only to contrast this with the views expressed by Lenin on this question in a clear-cut unequivocal manner. As Lenin said :

We are living, not merely in a state but in a system of states and the existence of the Soviet Republic side by side with imperialist states for a long time is unthinkable. One or the other must triumph in the end. And before that end supervenes a series of frightful collisions between the Soviet Republic and the bourgeois states would be inevitable. (Selected Works, Vol. VIII. p. 33)

The role of the Socialist Soviet Republic, which Lenin

106

envisaged in this historical background, also needs to be noted here:

The victorious proletariat (in the Socialist State) having expropriated the capitalists and organised its own Socialist production, would stand up against the rest of the capitalist world, attracting to its cause the oppressed classes of other countries, raising revolts in those countries, agonist the capitalists in the event of necessity coming out even with armed force against the exploiting classes and their states.[3] (Selected Works Vol. V. p. 141.)

'An arrant Nonsense'?

These words of Lenin, uttered two or three decades ago, however hardly concerns Zhdanov or induce him to take account of them in his formulation of the historic tasks confronting communists today. Thus it comes about even while urging fraternal Communist Parties outside Soviet Union to the task of "resistance to the plans of imperialist expansion and aggression of Anglo-American powers—along every line" in the background of the post war break-up of the People's war coalition.

Zhdanov rather takes good care to ensure that this resistance movement is conducted on the plane of anti-imperialism and national democracy alone and all references to the proletarian socialist revolution is scrupulously avoided.

Not only Mao Tse-Tung in China, but leading Stalinist spokesman in Western Europe and America as well, have never, in fact, concealed the fact that Socialist world revolution or the overthrow of capitalism is definitely outside the immediate historical perspective of Cominform and the Stalinist Communist Movement. Gilbert Green, the US Stalinist leader (one of the 12 Communist defendants involved in the recent Foley Square Trial in the USA) made this absolutely clear last year, in course of his theoretic polemic with Earl Browder—the P.C. Joshi of U.S. Stalinism—who referred by the way, to 'a

107

transition to Socialism' as an 'immediate task' in Western Europe. As an ardent Stalinist, Green was emphatically of the opinion that so far Western Europe was concerned, "transition to Socialism' was not the immediate task at all; but rather the "struggle for peace" against imperialist war mongers and against the colonising plans of US imperialism for the enslavement of Europe (the struggle for Socialism or a reference to a 'transition to Socialism' might prevent 'unity' with those "really patriotic elements" about whom Zhdanov speaks!). Even the very mild and basically reformist casual reference of Browder about 'transition to Socialism' as an immediate task therefore throws Green into hysterics. "This is arrant nonsense," asserts Green, 'Transition to Socialism is not the immediate issue in all Europe.

Thorez on Peace and National Independence

Stalinist leaders of France and Italy, like the famous Thorez and Palmiro Togliatti have also often, expressed themselves in almost identical terms at different times. Instead of 'Socialism' they would rather employ words like 'progressive democracy' 'popular democracy' 'liberty' 'national independence' etc., to describe the immediate political objectives of their parties. Thorez for example, in his recent speech to the Central Committee directs the members of the CP. France "to devote all their efforts to the development of a decisive struggle for peace and national independence." And again in conclusion he urges them to "the struggle for saving peace, for the restoration of national security of France, in defence of the liberties and the immediate demands of working people in order to create a democratic and independent France which will follow the path of Socialism;" but deliberately refrains from speaking of Socialist revolution straight away.

The following quotation from the 1946 post-election statement of Thorez, the French communist leader is also interesting in this connection :

The progress of democracy in the world, with few exceptions that confirm the rule, makes it possible to advance towards Socialism by other paths than those trodden by the Russian Communists. In any case, each country must choose its way. We have always thought and said that the people of France with her glorious tradition will find their own way towards more democracy, progress and social justice. (London Time, Nov. 18,1946).

No comment is perhaps necessary on this except that it admirably anticipated the Beirut conception of "gradual transition to Socialism without wide-spread civil war" etc., and the Gil Green conception of denial of the necessity of such transition in the immediate future by clever terminological sleights of hand with almost meaningless liberal democratic phrases about "more democracy", "more progress" and "more social justice."

Who are to be the partisans of the Democratic Camp

The camp that opposes Anglo-American imperialist Camp is therefore according to the Zhdanov formulation, the camp of world proletarian or Socialist revolution, but is deliberately termed by him as the "democratic" "anti-imperialist" Camp only, whose sole object is to defend "enduring peace and popular democracy," the "national Sovereignty and independence" of their countries! And obviously enough a national democratic movement of this nature does not rule out unity with "all really patriotic elements" belonging to other classes including considerable sections of the national bourgeoisie, who do not want their countries to be imposed upon by Anglo-American imperialists, who want to resist the imposition of their country by American monopolists and to uphold their "national honour and sovereignty." Such elements may conceivably even come from the capitalist class also. So just as in the "anti Fascist' People's War days, the entire movement against Anglo-American

109

imperialism must be kept hamstrung within a democratic nationalist framework and must not be allowed to overstep its limits; it must not speak of the overthrow of capitalism or of a Socialist revolution. And equally, as in those days, the entire world working-class movement in different countries must decide all "Key problems" that may confront them on by reference to the then foreign-policy line of the SU, and their tactical line "must revolve round the axis" of the defence and reinforcement of Soviet Union as Manuilisky had urged fifteen years ago.

Crusade against Anglo-America : Since

Zhdanov's address to the Cominform Conference made that amply clear. The CPSU and its leaders felt the necessity of organising resistance to the Anglo-American powers, he points out, only when "the British and American imperialist manifested their unwillingness to respect the legitimate interest of the Soviet Union and the democratic countries." For full two years after the close of war the Soviet Union had been following a policy "of consistently working for the observance of democratic principles in the post-war settlement." But the Council of Foreign Ministers held in March and April 1947 finally convinced the Soviet leadership that the US and Anglo-French imperialism had 'again' taken the path of imperialist expansion and aggression (as if they could ever be expected to take any other path!) and that America had abandoned "the old course of Roosevelt and passing to a new policy, the policy of preparing for new military adventures." It was also obvious to the Soviet leaders that this frankly aggressive and expansionist course to which Anglo-America, especially USA, had committed themselves, was directed principally against the Soviet Union. "Literally on the day, following the conclusion of World War II", complained Zhdanov, "they set to work to build up a front hostile to the USSR and World democracy." The entire world strategy of the CPSU and the world Stalinist movement had therefore to be recast in terms of organising

110

resistance to Anglo-America and their anti-Soviet War plans. That is the genesis and meaning of Zhdanov's call of resistance against Anglo-American imperialism in general and against American imperialism, in particular, in September 1947.

Logical out-come of power-politics

Taken the background of the overall denial of the perspective of Socialist revolution, not only in colonial countries but even in advanced capitalist countries of Western Europe, the deliberate substitution of the class-collaborationist Social reformist conception of a People's Democratic revolution in the place of Socialist revolution as the immediate goal of the movement in every country, the denial of the historic necessity of a revolutionary overthrow of capitalism and proletarian dictatorship as the inevitable transitional phase towards Socialism and the envisagement of the possibility of gradual evolution towards Socialism without any widespread civil war or the employment of violence, the Zhdanov line cannot but be regarded from the Leninist point of view as the inevitable outcome of Soviet power-politics against the USA (and also against Britain to the extent that Britain is allied to America). It does not hesitate to employ the nationalist-democratic mass opposition which is surging in various countries against Anglo-American imperialism after the termination of the war for strengthening or reinforcing its own policy-moves against USA or Great Britain without allowing such opposition movements to transcend the social reformist class-collaborationist limits of People's Democracy. Whatever might be the face-value of its tirades against Anglo American imperialism and the objective possibility of its unleashing mass-forces against imperialism in concrete political circumstances of particular countries, we cannot also shut our eyes to the basically reformist inhibitions of the entire movement, the possibility of its holding back the working-class and other revolutionary mass-forces from the path of militant class struggle against capitalism and other vested interests and from the path of Socialist revolution, as well as the possibility of its coming to terms with the ruling bourgeoisie in particular capitalist countries or any other action of the class, provided they agree to co-operate with Soviet State at least to move in the same direction in their foreign policy line as the Soviet Union.

Ample scope for shifts

The Zhdanov line never ruled out these possibilities. Not only that, it definitely left the scope wide open behind its apparent 'left' orientation for open collaboration and political coalitions with the ruling bourgeoisie in different countries or any other section of the bourgeoisie who might be in opposition for the present, but who might, some day, come into the government or might prove themselves powerful enough to bring to bear the pressure of their own influence upon the policies of the existing government, should the international foreign policy line and the national defence of Soviet Union against either of the Anglo-American powers demand such coalition. There was in other words ample theoretical and ideological scope within the frame-work of the general policy laid down by Zhdanov in September, 1947, for sharp changes to the left (provided these changes did not seek to mobilise mass force for a revolutionary class-struggle line for the overthrow of capitalism) as well as for sharp changes to the right (provided these did not mean unconditional surrender to the anti-Soviet 'imperialist' policies of America at-least, before the Soviet Union itself were prepared to alter and redefine its policies and attitude with regard to that power) according to the dictates of the foreign policy manoeuvres of the Soviet Union vis-a-vis Anglo-America. The original shift from 'right' to 'left' in the CPI line in 1948 had served its purpose and exhausted its practical utility. It was now time again to swing back to the right. The Zhdanov thesis did not forbid that.

Notes:

1. cf. —"The thirteen wicked men of Kremlin" according to Mr. Churchill.

2. Lest there be any misunderstanding on this score Manuilisky hastened to add that the prospect of world proletarian revolution and "the whole development of the world working class movement" was "inseparable from further victories of Socialism in USSR. —so that the working class movement in every country had for the present to reinforce the USSR further from the outside, as much as it lay in their power, and ensure further victories of Socialism in USSR. Only then would the base grow really strong and make further progress in the development of world working class movement concretely possible. There have been, of course, subsequent additions and elaborations in theory with regard to this question since 1935, which rule out the idea of a Proletarian Socialist Revolution or the revolutionary overthrow of capitalism in countries outside the USSR from the immediate historical perspective of Stalinist Communist Parties altogether." For that, see text further on in this chapter. The axial dictum of Manuilisky with regard to the 'reinforcement' of the USSR, however, continues unchanged. ('The work of the 7th Congress of Communist International-D. Z. Manuilisky: 'Peace Front' to People's War', P 248).

3. It has recently been argued that this programme was only "a possibility arising out of necessity"—the necessity of withstanding foreign military intervention etc.; and not a fundamental programme! (See Political Affairs February 1948; article by George Siskind, P 30-31.) It must not be thought that Lenin was against normal peaceful diplomatic relations or ordinary trade exchanges between the Soviet Union and the Capitalist States. That is not true. But his views about the historical significance of the Soviet State, its role in world affairs and the trend of world movement and forces with which it should be allied are beyond the scope of any misunderstanding.

Genesis of the Swing Back

The New India-Line

That the evaluation of the role of the India Government in the world affairs by the CPSU and international Stalinist leadership may have undergone any change in recent months and that the general attitude and policy line of the international Stalinist movement towards India and the India Government take a new orientation consequently need not however be deduced a *priori* from the assumption of an invariable connection between the national tactical line of Stalinist Communist Parties in different countries and the foreign policy of the Soviet Union, or from the mere fact of the peremptory Cominform directive to the CPI to change its line of tactics and general policy and throw out Ranadive in favour of the comparatively moderate Dange-Rajeswar Rao combine. As a matter of fact the Cominform Editorial did not even refer to the Nehru Government or Soviet attitude towards the matter. But sufficient indications have already appeared in the international Stalinist press pointing to such a change though in general the expression of the changed attitude has been very cautious and guarded so as not to create the impression that the CPSU or international Stalinism has suddenly become enamoured of the Government of Pandit Nehru or started to regard Pandit Nehru himself as a 'progressive' after the manner of P.C. Joshi. As we shall see, there is much in the policy as a matter of fact and more specifically in the foreign policy of Pandit Nehru which is not liked by and appears 'ambiguous' to the leaders of the Soviet Union and the Cominform. But in spite of this, an unmistakable change of tone is discernible, which can be directly linked up with the change of CPI tactical line in India. Instead of an attitude of direct hostility and overall condemnation, there were significant references to India by Soviet statesmen in a new tone of cordiality and friendliness, and the line of attack against Nehru Government's Foreign policy in party press became palpably mild and less critical than heretofore.

The background

In order to disabuse ourselves of any misunderstanding about such a change in the general attitude of the Stalinist Communist movement in the appraisal of a government condemned as a 'capitalist' and a 'satellite' collaborationist government till the other day, being possible at all, we have to keep our minds riveted on the basic world-outlook of Stalinism as discussed in the foregoing chapter, on its denial of the immediate historic perspective, or even the necessity, of the overthrow of capitalism or of calling for Socialist revolution in any country outside the frontiers of the USSR, and holding up in its stead the alternative perspective *of peaceful co-existence* of socialism and capitalism side by side, and on its insistence on the necessity of determining all key problems of the world working class movement by the criterion of defence and reinforcement of the USSR. Cooperation and alliance of Stalinist Communists in any country or countries outside Soviet Union, including India, was never precluded under terms of that basic outlook. The Zhdanov line of 1947 kept the way wide open, as we have seen, for such cooperation, and there is no reason to be surprised, if under the circumstances of to-day international Stalinist leadership find it advisable to show a certain degree of friendliness towards the Nehru Government in India and seek to find out fellow-travellers from a section or sections of Indian capitalists. The main consideration were the interests of Soviet foreign policy.[1]

Altered balance offerees in East Asia

It has been indicated above in broad outlines how the actual need for a re-orientation of Stalinist tactics and the swing back from the left to the right, arose towards the close of the last year.

Briefly, it was the direct result of the following factors.

116

(1) A radical alteration in the international balance of powers in East Asia and the Pacific after the defeat of Chiang Kai-Shek and the US-backed KMT nationalists and the emergence of the frankly pro-Soviet Chinese People's Republic with unchallenged control over the entire vast expanse of Chinese mainland.

(2) A sharp increase of Anglo-American contradictions and conflict of interests in West Europe, Middle East and South East Asia and the open divergence of British and US policies with regard to the People's Republic of China and East Asian pro-Soviet bloc.

(3) The general line-up of Nehru's India with the British Commonwealth in all larger matters of world-policy and especially with regard to the recognition of People's China, which meant that Nehru Government's policy in East Asia would diverrge from that of USA at hast to the extent of Britain's, correspondingly weakening and undermining US-Far East strategy and favouring SU at the expense of US.

(4) The frantic efforts of the Nehru Government in between Anglo-America and the Soviet Union, to seek the way to an effective *modus vivendi* of its own, in order to safeguard the basic structure of the vested interests of the class and classes it represents, in the background of the general breakdown of the imperialist capitalist system and the revolutionary upsurge of the toiling masses, by coming to terms with decidedly reformist trends in the popular movement and their leadership before it was too late. An understanding with the Chinese People's Republic and the Chinese Communists with their theory of new democracy, and with the entire pro-Soviet bloc of East Asia, might yet provide the Nehru Government with such a *modus vivendi,* which means in effect that the Nehru Government would have to readjust its international relationship with the Soviet Union and the Soviet Bloc of countries correspondingly.

117

India recognises Chinese People's Republic

Recognition of the People's Republic of China by the Nehru Government, in the face of decided American opinion against it marked the decisive beginning of this process of readjustment. It should only be remembered in this connection that Nehru's India, no less than Great Britain, is still very largely dependent on USA financially and economically. The hostility of the ruling classes of these countries to Communism or Soviet Socialism (if not to the Soviet State as such), and to any indication of genuinely progressive and revolutionary mass-upsurges in their own territories were no less real. Similarly real were their apprehensions and fears against the phenomenal increase of the strength and influence of the USSR in the post-war period. There is therefore bound to be a good deal of hesitancy and equivocation about the entire attitude of Nehru Government in its relationship with the Russo-Chinese camp and the American camp, an a good deal of self-contradiction will necessarily be inherent in its whole position. Moreover, leaving aside USA, the opposition of Great Britain itself and the British Commonwealth of Nations, with which India has been linked up by Pandit Nehru's Government, towards the SU and the pro-Soviet People's democratic camp, is also a factor of considerable significance and is invariably reflected in the foreign policy of the India Government, which is guided from behind the scenes by the hardened British stooge Girija Shankar Bajpai. But nevertheless the recognition of the People's Republic of China by India and the advocacy by India for the admission of the former's representatives to the UNO and its Security Council is a move running positively counter to American Far Eastern policies and strengthens and reinforces the Soviet Union's diplomatic position as against USA. The importance of such a move, at such a time, by the government of the leading Asian country outside the Soviet bloc, a government which apparently came to power in the postwar period on the crest of a popular mass movement and still had a very great influence over the minds of the masses, and a government which the American imperialists had hoped to press into service as their last line of defence and their last buttress in Asia after their total strategic debacle in China, is self-evident.

Difference between Britain's and India's recognition of New China.

The difference between the British recognition of the Chinese People's Republic and that by India could not also be lost sight of by the discerning eye of the Soviet leaders. The former was partly the result of Anglo-American conflicts of imperialist interest and policies in the Pacific and South East Asian region, and partly the result of an inordinate eagerness on the part of crisis-ridden British imperialism to salvage a part at least of its vast stakes in Chinese trade and commerce. Britain was even encouraged to entertain hopes for a sizable share in the economic and industrial development that might be undertaken by the new government and in meeting new China's demand for capital goods by the eminently 'reasonable' attitude which the Chinese Communists were inclined to take about private capitalism and the trading rights of foreign and Chinese nationals. But India evidently did not have as yet any such clash of imperialist and finance-capitalistic interests with USA in the Eastern market. Nor, did it have such extensive trading interests in China that tempted Britain.

Basic weakness of the Indian bourgeoisie

The major consideration behind India's decision about the recognition of the Peking Republic was the necessity felt by the new rulers of India of submitting to the *fait accompli* and adjust themselves as far as possible to the new situation created by the release of revolutionary mass forces in East Asia by the mighty impetus of Japanese war and post-war crisis of the colonial system. The inherent weakness in the position of the Indian bourgeoisie, who were increasingly feeling the irresistible impact of a growing restiveness of the masses below

119

their feet, inevitably led them in search of a surer prop than Chiang Kai-Shek ever had, in the shape of possible alliances and understandings with the leadership of the rising mass forces beyond their own borders in those countries at least where popular forces had come to power, and where the leadership of the mass movements still preferred, in spite of their open pro-Soviet affiliations, to keep themselves delimited within the frame-work of a petty-bourgeois social reformist policy with only vague orientations towards Socialism. Due to this basic weakness of their policy it might be possible to persuade them, by combining the tactics of judicious takling on the diplomatic level with the employment, as occasion arose, of the pressure of restricted mass-agitation from below, to maintain quite friendly relations with the Sino-Soviet bloc in the Far East, if not to join it formally. They might under certain circumstances be induced to throw their weight in favour of the former against USA in world affairs.

The new India-line set-forth

(I) *A speech by Vyshinsky*

That some such move for tackling the Indian bourgeoisie might have been actually underway after the anouncement of India's recognition of the Chinese People's Republic, was first indicated indirectly by Soviet Foreign Minister Vyshinsky's speech in the banquet given by Ambassador Radhakrishnan at Moscow for celebrating the inauguration of the 'Republican' constitution of India on the 26th of January last. Vyshinsky was reported to have greeted the establishment of the Indian Republic as "a most important step in advance" in modern times, at the very time, be it remembered, when the left parties of India-including the CPI were holding mass meetings and other forms of political demonstrations, protesting against the promulgation of an authoritarian semi-fascist Constitution modelled on the hated Government of India Act of 1935 in the name of freedom and secular democracy; (See : full report of the speech as reproduced in Hindu, Jan. 31. 1950)

(a) *The Tokuda formulation : "India cannot ignore liberation movements"*

That this was not just an usual expression of 'diplomatic' politeness on the occasion of a formal state-ceremony in the accredited embassy of another state, but might also be taken as the pointer to a new orientation of the India-policy of the CPSU for the entire Stalinist movement, was amply proved by a radically new analysis about the foreign policy of India that was given by Kyiuchi Tokuda, General Secretary of Communist Party of Japan a few days earlier, and which was duly reproduced in Soviet Press and also in the official Cominform organ 'Lasting Peace.'

Tokuda remarked :

The neutral attitude taken by India is explained by the fact that India cannot ignore the popular liberation movement in the countries of South-East Asia. Thus the setting up of an anti-Communist front headed by India is impossible. This meant in other words that the Congress Government in India and Pandit Jawaharlal Nehru would not play the role of K.MT or Chiong Kai-Shek, and fight US imperialism's counterrevolutionary battles in S.E. Asia, but would rather prefer to come to terms with the revolutionary forces headed by the Chinese Communist Party and the Soviet. This was of course put down to the financial and other weaknesses of Indian capitalists. But this new interpretation of Nehru Governments' policy of "neutrality" between rival power blocs, taken together with the significant remarks of Vyshinsky's felicitation speech about the Republic of India undoubtedly sounds like an anti-climax after the virulent condemnation hurled against Pandit Nehru by leading colonial national-liberation movements experts and India experts in Soviet Union like Zhukov et. al. till the other day.

121

Only six months back!

"The Indian bourgeoisie"[2] now rivals the "most reactionary forces in stifling the mass popular movement," asserted Zhukov only six months back in June 1949, "in the terror against the progressive elements of the working class and peasant movements. The metamorphosis, of Nehru from a left Congressite and an accuser of imperialism into a shrewd servant of two masters both Britain and USA is a clear demonstration of this" (June 8, 1949 'Problems of National and Colonial Struggle After the War').

Parallel with this there came the satirical appraisal of Nehru Government's "Independent" and "neutral" foreign policy as being designed only "for duping the popular masses' and for 'deceiving public opinion both in India and abroad" by V. Balabushevich and others.

"In actual practice the reactionary circles in India" remarked Balabushevich "were adopting a course of consolidating the position of their country in role of satellites of the Anglo-American imperialist bloc" ('New Stage in the National Liberation Movement of the People of India' *Problem of Economics,* Moscow; No. 8) The contrast here is too obvious to need any comment!

Significance of Tokuda line

The special significance of the new analysis of Nehru Government's foreign policy as given by Tokuda, as the General Secretary of the Japanese Communist Party, arises from the fact that the political line of policy and the tactics for CP. Japan were being determined for sometimes past under the direct supervision of the Communist Party of the Soviet Union and the Cominform, and generally had the direct sanction of the Soviet leadership. Since the concentration of the US efforts, after big-scale American strategic reverses in China, on feverishly building up Japan as the principal war-base against USSR in the Far East, the Communist party of Japan has acquired a particular importance in the eyes of CPSU leadership. Moreover, it is clearly evident that without the approval of the international leadership and the Cominform, Tokuda's Report could not in any case have been reproduced in the LPPD more than three months back after its original publication in January 24 in the *Akahata,* the organ of CP. Japan, at a time when the CPI itself was in the throes of an ideological and political confusion about the line to be adopted in India. As a matter of fact the Vyshinsky speech and the simultaneous publication of this new formulation about Nehru's foreign policy was a definite pointer to the CPI ranks for changing their tactics accordingly, from one of all-out opposition to that of the strengthening and fostering its new trend viz. its willingness of coming to terms with the 'revolutionary' forces, a trend evinced by the recognition of the Chinese People's Republic.

The recognition seemed to 'prove' negatively at least that India would not play the part of the spearhead of counter-revolution in South East Asia and pull America's chestnut out of fire!

The only 'correct' line of tactics which was to be adopted in this background was clearly indicated by the Cominform Editorial of January 27th. Henceforth the Indian Communists must give up their policy of barren opposition and "must unite with all classes, parties, groups and organizations willing to defend the national independence and freedom of India." From now-on the main brunt of the struggle had to be turned mainly against imperialism, and their feudal and big bourgeois collaborators incidentally, but certainly not against those who were coming to terms with revolutionary forces and refused to set up an anti-Communist front at the bidding of American imperialism.

The Vyshinsky speech, the Tokuda line about Nehru Government's foreign policy with a seal of sanction from the international leadership and the new Cominform directive all three logically followed from a reorientated policy line and were the clearest indications of a definite change of basic CPSU appraisal of the role of India and the Indian Government under Nehru which automatically made a change in CPI tactics imperative and a disavowal of the much-boosted 'leftism' of Ranadive as a 'left-deviation' inevitable.

Critical ambiguity of a Berezhkov

This should not be taken to mean however, that the foreign policy manoeuvres of the India Government were to be regarded from now onwards as entirely satisfactory from the point of view of the CPSU, or that the CPI would be required to give up its crtical attitude to the Nehru Government and its foreign policy line. There was much in that policy which was not at all to the liking of the CPSU and the international Stalinist leadership. Neither could India's recognition of the People's Republic of China be regarded as entirely voluntary. It was clearly forced on the Nehru Government by the radical alteration in international balance of powers after the victory of the Chinese People's Liberation Army. India's affiliations with the British Commonwealth, and through it to the United States, was too obtrusively palpable to be ignored altogether. India Government might yet be drawn into an open alliance with US against the Soviet-led 'democratic camp.' It was prevented from "leaning towards the United States" as per G.D. Birla's advice only owing to "the fear of their own people" and the "powerfully surging movement for national liberation throughout Asia and Far East." It was also due to the weakness of India's general position in the present world set-up. The line of official party criticism about Nehru Government's foreign policy and its entanglements with Anglo-American imperialism was recently set forth in some detail in an article in the Soviet weekly, *New Times* (no 22, May 1950) specially written by the Soviet publicist V. Berezhkov. The most curious thing about this article which apparently spoke very sharply about the Congress Government's "compact with the imperialists" and their increasing "surrender" to the "extortionate demands of the

Anglo-American imperialists," is however that it was more concerned to prove that "there was a good deal of *ambiguity*" about the so-called "middle course" and policy of "neutrality" of the India Government, and that the Indian leaders were "wary of openly associating" with the aggressive pacts proposed by US imperialism. A good deal *of ambiguity* came therefore to characterise the seemingly caustic criticism of Nehru's foreign policy by Comrade Berezhkov. "More and more" wrote Berezhkov, "India's ruling circles are abandoning the defence of national interests"... "Britain follows in the wake of Washington's aggressive policy, and India top trims her sails to suit the American imperialists." But due note was taken, at the same time, that the leaders of the Indian National Congress are displaying greater caution than their American partners would like "and that Pandit Nehru resented to the crude pressure" that he was subjected to in Washington! Apparently Indian leaders though prepared to barter away some of the country's vital interests to the Wall Street were wary of openly associating themselves with it "They have learnt a lesson" he concluded, "from the inglorious fate of the Kuomintang clique!"

Terms of Complaint against Nehru The main terms of the complaint against Nehru Government which were detailed by him were the following :

1) hampering the development of trade relations with the Soviet Union and the People's Democracies;

2) sending a delegate to the Baguio anti-Communist Conference convened by President Quirino of Philippines after initial announcement of an intention of non-participation in it;

3) taking an 'evasive' stand at the British Empire Conference at Sydney ('evasive' against what?) :

4) helping anti-popular regimes in Asia, notably the government of Thakin Nu in Burma;

5) taking an *ambiguous* stand on the representation of the Chinese People's Republic in the UN;

6) brutal persecution of 'democrats' in India.

The new line of agitation against Nehru's foreign policy

These were in effect a sort of suggestion from CPSU about the line of agitation along which pressures were to be brought against Nehru Government's foreign policy the implication being that Nehru would be deemed respectable if his government removes these 'evasions' and 'ambiguities.' It was particularly noted therefore that the Indian rulers feared popular resistance and were perhaps amenable to it, that India was 'one of the weakest links in the imperialist chain." So if a vigorous mass agitation could be got up against the Indian Government and public opinion mobilized on these lines (not on lines of mis-conceived 'militant mass actions' of the Ranadive Period) it might not be entirely impossible to draw away India and the Nehru Government from their present imperialist moorings nearer to the people's democratic camp.

The departure

Thus the need of criticism against Nehru's policy was still there from the Stalinist point of view. But the criticism would have to be cautious, realistic and imaginative enough to take note of India Government's hesitations about allying themselves openly with the American bloc, and also take advantage of these hesitations. That was the clear hint of Berezhkov in his *ambiguous* criticism of Nehru's *ambiguities.*

Whatever might be one's views about Nehru's ambiguities there is hardly any room for doubt that Berezhkov's own ambiguities about Nehru are a clear departure from the earlier Zhukov-Balabushevich line of down-right condemnation of Pandit Nehru's Government, as direct and open collaborators of Anglo-American imperialism and "as the servant of two masters Britain and the USA." The reasons for this departure have, however, been amply dealt with above.

Post script

The foregoing section was written in the main before the new developments in connection with the Korean War took place. US intervention in Korea, the respective stands of the British and India Governments on the UNO resolution on Korea, Pandit Nehru' peace proposals to Marshal Stalin and President Truman and the welcome accorded to them by Stalin as well as the curt refusal of USA all these have amply confirmed the conclusions reached above. The announcement of whole-hearted support to Pandit Nehru's move by the recently released Stalinist leader Dange comes as a logical sequel. It now seems that active support of the claim of the Chinese People's Republic to UNO representation by Pandit Nehru and India's vote in favour of Soviet representative M. Jacob Malik's proposal in Security Council for unseating the delegate of Nationalist China from that body have actually removed a major item of 'ambiguity' in India Government's foreign policy against which Berezhkov complained so much! One of the recent issues of the LPPD (No. 30, July 28)the Comminform organ makes the following Editorial comment about the new foreign policy of the Indian bourgeoisie, after Pt. Nehru's peace proposals :

The very fact of the peaceable initiative displayed by a number *of bourgeois* newspapers and politicians who have come out in favour of accepting the proposals of J.V. Stalin, testify to the fact that *the most sober minds among the bourgeoisie* are beginning to show serious uneasiness with regard to the consequences of the adventurous policy of war provocations being pursued by US imperialist.

The editorial remarks of the LPPD amply testifies in its turn to the fact that the international Stalinist assessment about the Indian bourgeoisie have also been changing rather 'seriously'! The significance of the Soviet and Stalinist point of view of the "peaceable initiative" of Nehru and the "uneasiness" shown by "sober minds among the bourgeoisie" in India at US war provocation has also been made sufficiently clear in this

127

article : "The US-British ruling circles are dissatisfied," point out the Cominform Editorial Board, "with Nehru's action..."

In view of the sharpened war danger, and the switch over of the US imperialists to direct acts of aggressive war, a further strengthening of the democratic camp and the consolidation of the forces of peace are of exceptional importance.

The hint is clear support the "peaceable initiative" of "sober bourgeois minds" by the "extension in every way of the mass basis of peace movement" and "drawing in of the broad peasant masses, middle urban strata, women and youth, and of all sections of the intelligentsia" etc.

One has only to recall in this connection E.M. Zuhkov's criterion of judging the "reactionary" or "progressive" nature of a colonial bourgeoisie by reference to its attitude towards the Soviet Union and the "democratic camp" to understand which way the wind is blowing.

Notes

1. The following quotation from the summing up lecture of E.M. Zhukov (one of the leading Soviet experts on India) to the three day's joint session of the Academic Councils of the Institute of Economics and the Pacific Institute of the Academy of Sciences, USSR, devoted to post-war national liberation struggles in the "colonies and semi-colonies (among which India is included) is very instructive. "Everywhere (India included) the main enemy of the national liberation movement is American imperialism. This is precisely why it is impossible to regard the national liberation movement of every individual country...apart from its connection with the struggle of the two camps, the struggle of the forces of democracy and Socialism (SU i.e.) against the forces of imperialism and reaction (USA and its allies or collaborators). "The progressive character of this or that social movement, the revolutionary or reactionary nature of this or that party at the present time is determined by its attitude towards the Soviet Union........Therefore, the controversy as to at what stage the colonial bourgeoisie

(here, Nehru Government) begins to play a reactionary role can be solved only under the circumstances when an answer is given to the main question" (Colonial People's Struggle For Liberation, PPH. P. 99).

The long and short of Zhukov's argument as concretely applied to India means that at what stage Nehru Government can be said to play a reactionary role, has to be decided not by reference to his actual social and political policies, but by reference to his attitude towards SU vis-a-vis USA. That is the crucial question or the 'axis' here also. It is equally applicable to every other sections of the Indian bourgeoisie.

2. The attention of the discerning reader is here drawn to the fact that here as else where Zhukov also uses the generic term 'Indian bourgeoisie' in the manner of Ranadive instead of 'big bourgeoisie', although like Ranadive he also often employed the terms 'bourgeoisie' and 'big bourgeoisie' inter-changeably, But Ranadive is summarily thrown out as a 'left-deviationist' for having confused between the entire 'national bourgeoisie' and the 'big bourgeoisie' while Zhukov's speech still remains a Party text! V.M. Maslennikov also terms Nehru Govt a 'bourgeois' instead of a 'big bourgeois' Government.

Rationale for the Swing Back

Fresh advances Towards The Indian Bourgeoisie

In the new international set up of today — in the background of the altered correlationship of forces arising out of the increasing contradiction and conflicts of interest in the Anglo-American imperialist camp and the corresponding weakness and instability of the Indian bourgeoisie feeling threatened by the challenge of the rising mass-forces in India and South East Asia—the practical exigencies of Soviet foreign policy line, which determines the international tactical line for all Stalinist Communist party, demands a new mode of approach, tentatively at least, for tackling the ruling, Indian bourgeoisie. The Indian bourgeoisie have been compelled, as we have seen, to seek its own way to come to terms with the Sino-Soviet bloc to a certain extent in order to safeguard the basic structure of its own vested interests in this country without breaking off at the same time too radically from its Anglo-American moorings. It is apparent to the Indian bourgeoisie that it will have to forge out a *modus vivendi* by somehow coming to an understanding with the Sino-Soviet bloc. This has naturally offered a new opportunity from the Soviet point of view to get its own foreign policy line vis-a-vis Anglo-American imperialism reinforced with the support of Indian for whatever it is worth. It has become urgently necessary therefore for the international Stalinist movement to give up the previous policy of negation and total opposition to the Indian bourgeoisie and make cautious advances toward them and to ask the CPI recast its policies accordingly.

Requirements of an United Front

The ruling section of the bourgeoisie may not be immediately willing to enter into an open alliance with the Sino-Soviet bloc in Asia because of their previous commitments to Anglo-American imperialism and specific entanglements

131

with the empire-policies of the British Commonwealth. But there are other sections of the bourgeoisie who might be. Even the ruling section will be inclined to accord a greater weight to agreements in favour of aligning India with the Sino-Soviet bloc, if it finds that the opinion of a growing section of its own class including the middle and petty bourgeoisie, and the people in general, are strongly in favour of such an alignment. But in order to bring the bourgeoisie — ruling or non-ruling, 'big' or non-'big', 'pro-imperialist', 'potentially' anti-imperialist and 'anti imperialist'— round to that position, three essential requirements have to be fulfilled:

(1) they must be convinced in the first place, that it is essentially in their own interests (i.e. their own bourgeois class interests in the commercial and industrial development of India and the expansion of their overseas markets) that they must come closer to the Sino-Soviet bloc :

(2) they must be assured that the basic structure of capitalist vested-interests and capitalist property-relations are not in immediate jeopardy, or are not threatened by any "Moscow inspired" anti-capitalist or Socialist revolution fomented by 'Russian agents" i.e., by the Stalinist Communists here: and lastly,

(3) the bourgeoisie (both in and out of the ruling circle) must be reassured that the Communists here would not take an entirely negative and disruptionist attitude towards the Government of the day, (whichever party may be in power) or undermine its administrative structure as expressed in the past two years by any kind of disruptive tactics or armed insurrection but would be prepared to renounce those tactics openly and come back to the constitutional-political arena and co-operate with parties with whom they might agree on the policy level. It is only on this basis that the formation of a "united-front" with the "national" bourgeoisie would be possible and advantage could be taken of the situation where the Indian bourgeoisie are evincing an increasing eagerness for an

132

independent understanding and alignment with the Sino-Soviet bloc in preference to their unilateral reliance on the Anglo-American imperialist bloc as hitherto.

In the overall plan of resistance to Anglo-American imperialism within the framework of US-Soviet power politics — that is the essence of the new political stand which the Indian Communist party is inevitably called upon to take by its international leadership to-day.

Throwing out of Ranadive, condemnation of the Calcutta Thesis, tirade against the newly discovered 'left-sectarian', 'opportunist' Trotskyist deviations of the line followed blindly and unquestioningly during the past two years (because that line had at that time the hall-mark of 'international' approval and sanction from international Stalinist leadership), the orgy of penitent self-criticism, glorification of Mao and *China-way,* loud blares about the "correct policy" of Mao "in dealing with the national bourgeoisie," and the Mao conception of "united dictatorship of several anti-imperialist classes including the national bourgeoisie", advocacy of the necessity of allowing capitalism to continue for a long period to come in the name of an anti-imperialist and anti-feudal People's Democratic Revolution, total denial of the immediate historic perspective of the overthrow of capitalism or that of a Socialist revolution — all these logically follow as inevitable consequences from that basic position viz: United front with the national bourgeoisie.

Pre-1948 United Front in a new form

United front with the national bourgeoisie was the essence of the political line of the CPI in the pre-1948 days under Joshi. From People's War united front with British imperialism the party then stepped down a rung in the ladder and sought alliance with the Congress Leadership and the bourgeoisie who coming into power in the crest of a popular mass upsurge by entering into a backdoor compromisist deal with the British Government.

How Joshi came to grief

United Front with the Congress leadership basking in the full glory of national adulation by the naively trustful masses of the people — would be surest way, Joshi had hoped, to politically rehabilitate CPI in the eyes of the masses. But he forgot that the new alliance that was forged between the Indian bourgeoisie and Anglo-American imperialism on the basis of the so-called 'transfer of power' and 'independence' was primarily directed agaist the USSR and the democratic 'people's camp', and that Anglo-American imperalism had already *deserted* the 'camp of the people.' He forgot, in other words, that it was impossible for the People's War coalition to continue for long in the post-war period and could not foresee that the fact of its break-up was soon going to be announced by Zhdanov who would lay down an over-all plan of resistance to Anglo-American (or more precisely American) imperialism. The indiscretion committed by Joshi constituted the fact of his eagerness to rehabilitate the party politically after People's War betrayal by currying favour with the Congress leadership and thus he carried forward the understanding of the war-period to the post-war, which inevitably came into conflict with the requirements of Soviet foreign policy in the background of the growing estrangement, power-rivalry and hostility between Anglo-America and the USSR. Joshi was therefore made to take leave with the slur of reformism labelled on his head.

Basis of Joshi-ite 'Reformism'

United front with the bourgeoisie — that precisely was the essence of Joshi-ite reformism also. How did this reformism find expression? "After the partition of India" points out Maslennikov (another leading India-expert of the CPSU), the "leadership of the Communist Party took the decision to support the bourgeois" (mark, not big bourgeois) "Nehru Government

134

and decided on the 'expediency' of forming *a united national front* from Gandhi to the Communists." "This reformist line was strongly criticised and condemned" he adds with evident approval, in the Second Congress of the Communist Party of India which took place in February-March, 1948." both Ranadive and Joshi now seem to be agreed that it was an essentially 'opportunistic' 'class-collaborationist 'Menshevik' line, a line of complete surrender to bourgeois nationalism and nothing else (for Joshi's opinions on his own past mistakes see : Views No. 1). After the 'leftist' hay-fever of the past two years and playing with the tactics of combining the "most elementary" forms of struggle with the "most advanced," petition filing before Industrial Tribunals with wielding of arms in the Telengana way essentially in the hope of pushing the masses to the position where they will echo the party's slogan for ending the bourgeois governments," after two years of continuous encouragement from the international leadership in their fight against the government of the bourgeoisie, the party is now being told to change its tactics and form a broad "nationwide united front" with "all classes, parties and groups willing to defend the national independence and freedom of India" including the national bourgeoisie.

Allies abounding

There will be fight henceforth against Anglo-American imperialists alone, also against the "reactionary" big bourgeoisie (presumably there may be some "progressive" big-bourgeois groups.[1] still lurking here and there; or it may be that some of the big-bourgeois leaders who have been playing a reactionary role uptil now may turn progressive. But in any case, it is specifically the "reactionary" ones who will have to be fought, and feudal princes who are collaborating with the imperialists — but not against "national bourgeoisie" as such) or their government. The "national bourgeoisie" who are collaborating with imperialism are to be treated "as an ally" as Li Li-San pointed out in his speech before the Trade Union Conference of

Asian and Australasian countries in Peking last November!

Even Nehru may walk in!

The Cominform directive does not of course ask the Indian Communists to support the Nehru Government specifically or immediately enter into an united front with the Congress leaders as Joshi did in 1947. The Cominform apparently puts forward unexceptionable suggestions about forming 'a nation-wide united-front' with all anti-imperialist classes in the China fashion. It quotes Liu Shao-Chi only to emphasize that the path taken by Chinese people under the leadership of Mao Tse-Tung and the Chinese Communist Party, is the path that should be taken by the people of India and the Indian Communist Party also. This is apparently all. But the pointer is clear. Consult Mao, follow the China-way and find out your allies from the rich peasants, petty-bourgeoisie, important sectors of the middle bourgeoisie, even from willing big-bourgeois groups also if opportunity arises in the fight against America and Anglo-America and their collaborators in the fight for the defence of the "national independence and freedom of India." For, has not Mao definitely said that "the new democratic revolution is to eliminate only feudalism and monopoly capitalism, only the landlord class and the bureaucratic bourgeoisie (collaborating with imperialism) — not capitalism in general". and that" it will be still necessary to permit the existence, for a long period of the capitalist economy represented by the broad petty-bourgeoisie and the middle bourgeoisie even after the nation wide victory of the revolution"?

Then how can you exclude any body or any section of the bourgeoisie at this stage — when the nation-wide victory of revolution has not yet been achieved in India

Why Nehru was not named?

There are good reasons too why Nehru or the Congress

Government of India has not been mentioned by name openly as possible allies. In the first place it should be remembered that the position of Nehru Government is still "ambiguous" to a great extent in the Stalinist point of view (Berezhkov) owing to its past Anglo-American affiliation which it has not yet cut off. In the second place, Zhukov has clearly pointed out that "the progressive character of this or that social movement, revolutionary or reactionary nature of this or that party is at the present time determined by its attitude, towards the Soviet Union, to the camp of democracy and Socialism." Zhukov specifically applied this criterion in the case of the colonial bourgeoisie. "The controversy as to at what stage the colonial bourgeoisie begins to play a reactionary role" (or a revolutionary role), "can be solved only" under the conditions when an answer is given to this main question —" i.e. attitude towards the SU. The attitude of the Indian Communists to a united front with Nehru and the Congress Government will as a matter of course be decided concretely as concrete circumstances arise. But the way cannot be barred by obstinately and dogmatically clinging to the formulation of the Second Congress thesis of the CPI that henceforth "every step forward of the popular struggle is to be taken not only in opposition to imperialism but in opposition to the bourgeoisie also."

Nehru may not immediately come in the "broad nation-wide United front." Moreover, the question of extending all-out support to Nehru will not in any case arise till Nehru makes his attitudes less "ambiguous" with regard to the 'democratic' camp.

Back to Joshi line in a new form

But if the entire "national" bourgeoisie is included in the enemy camp along with imperialism, and if the threat is held out that the people's Democratic revolution will be directed not only against the Anglo-American imperialist camp but also for the 'simultaneous' building up of Socialism, then not only will

137

no ally be found from the ranks of the big bourgeoisie, but also middle bourgeoisie and petty-bourgeosie will not be inclined to come. So the line of the Calcuta thesis has to be scrapped now in the interest of a "broad nationwide united front" with the "national" bourgeoisie. The only difference between this "broad nation-wide united front" suggested by the Cominform Editorial and the pre-1948 "united national front" advocated by Joshi is that instead of employing the abstract class term (an algebraic term one may say) 'national bourgeoisie', Joshi mentioned Nehru Government and the Congress leaders by name—without taking into account Nehru Government's affiliations with Anglo-America and the two-camp division of the world and without putting forward before that Government the crucial categorical demand for entering into a closer alliance with the Soviet camp. But there is absolutely no fundamental difference from the point of view of its class content.

In search of capitalist fellow-travellers

In order to direct the minds of the CPI ranks to the necessity of seeking, "fellow travellers" from the camp of the 'national bourgeoisie' as distinguished from its ruling section, clear hints have been thrown by Soviet India experts from time to time as to the particular capitalist groups who might come with them and may support them against the government (provided the movement is directed against imperialism and feudalism only and not against capitalism as such or the capitalist class). Based on A. M. Dyakov's thesis that the agreement between British imperialism and Indian big bourgeoisie was an alliance of the former with Gujrati and Marwari capitalist alone the suggestion was developed that individual groupings from the national bourgeoisie particularly those of other nationalities whose interests are adversely affected by the alliance between foreign capital and the Gujrati-Marwari group might be brought in. The first self-critical statement of the Ranadivite Polit-Bureau after publication of the Cominform Editorial expressed its willingness to explore these

138

possibilities. As a typical instance of the lines on which the party's mind is working, the sudden anxiety displayed by the Bengal Provincial Committee of the CPI in their criticism of the PB about the ruin of Bengali banks and Bengali trade and industries in the "unequal competition" with *Tatas* and Birlas (although the Tatas are neither Gujrati nor a *Marwari* firm) may be cited (Bengal PC statement of 14.4.50). In other words attempts will be made from now onwards to bring the dissatisfied and disgruntled Bengali bankers and industrialists (and their counterparts in other provinces) in the "broad nation-wide united front" to the formation of which the Cominform Editorial Board directs the Indian Communists. It is easy to see that distinction between this united front and the united national front advocated by Joshi would be less than that between tweedle-dum and tweedle-dee, but for the 'ambiguous' foreign policy manoeuvres of Nehru against which Berezhkov complains. If Nehru cares to remove those ambiguities and brings India nearer to the Sino-Soviet bloc then perhaps even the 'bourgeois' Nehru Government would not remain untouchable for long.

In the meantime we may expect to witness ardent Communist pleadings for Bengali banking and Bengali industrial development, a sight which would be worth even for the gods to see!

Theoretical plea

All this is being done on the specious theoretical plea-advanced with authoritative citations from Stalin and Mao Tse-tung that India *is still a colonial country* with ruling power concentrated in the hands of British imperialism and native princes and their big bourgeois collaborators, and the struggle in India is primarily a *colonial national liberation* struggle where the *'national"* bourgeoisie or a section of it 'may for some time' play a revolutionary role (Stalin).

That the colonial bourgeoisie may under certain

circumstances play a progressive role, to a certain limited extent, with regard to the national liberation struggle in colonial and dependent countries is however elementary Marxism-Leninism. The strangest part of the whole affair is that these ABC principles are being hurled at the party now after so many years! Quotations are lifted from Stalin's writings of 25 years ago in order to prove that the Indian bourgeoisie is *now* split into two sections as Stalin had foreseen—the treacherous reformist section represented by the 'big' bourgeoisie who are collaborating with imperialism and had entered into a bloc with imperialism against the workers and peasants of their own country, and the revolutionary section and from that premise is deduced the necessity of concentrating fire on the compromising and collaborationist section of the national bourgeoisie and entering into a united front with the revolutionary section.

What Stalin said in 1925?

The particular passage which is often referred to in this connection occurs in Stalin's address to the University of the Toilers of the East at Taskhent in May, 1925. His speech had particular reference to conditions obtaining in different colonial countries *then,* i.e., 1925, nearly three decades back from to-day.

It should be particularly noted that Stalin was at that time especially concerned to emphasize the difference in the political situation and class alignments of different colonial countries and the tasks that confronted the respective Communist Parties of those countries at that time, in the different concrete set up of their respective countries.

Briefly, he divided the colonial countries into three categories (I) industrially undeveloped colonies, like Morocco, which have almost no proletariat and where the national bourgeoisie had yet no grounds for splitting into a revolutionary party and a compromising party; (2) countries like China and

140

Egypt, which were industrially less developed with a comparatively small proletariat, and where the bourgeoisie was split, but the compromising section had not as yet welded itself to imperialism; and (3) *capitalistically developed* colonies like India, where the compromising section had treachrously gone over to imperialism and formed bloc with the latter. He wanted the Communists in India to form a united front — "a national revolutionary anti-imperialist bloc" — the working class would try to ensure its hegemony step by step by dislodging the bourgeoisie from the position of leadership over the liberation movement.

The situation then and now

It will be evident to everybody that Stalin's analysis had direct relevance to conditions when a split occurred in the Indian National Congress after the Constitutional reforms introduced by the British Government in 1918-19, the break-away of the moderate leaders from the Congress and the formation of the Liberal Party which entered into direct collaboration with British imperialism, on the basis of sham Diarchical Reforms in the provincial sphere. It will also be evident that this split, or the subsequent split in the leadership of the Congress between the Gandhians and the Swarajists after the collapse of the non-cooperation movement and the betrayal of the bourgeois leadership of the Congress in 1921, or the going over of a handful political leaders from the top-notch section of big bourgeois representatives to the side of imperialism without any semblance of a share in actual political power (which was concentrated in the hands of irresponsible imperialist bureaucrats) and the going-over of the major bourgeois party in the country viz: the Congress (as well as the Liberals) to an alliance with British imperialism on the basis of formal transfer of power and the international recognition of India as an independent Sovereign State in 1947, do not stand on the same par, either politically or socio-historically. This 'transfer of power' has, it is true, given the *masses* of Indian

141

people no more than a semblance of independence. It has not been in any sense a transfer of power (the right of self-determination) to the *masses* of the people or *their* freedom. But the substantial legal and constitutional reality of the transfer of power *to the bourgeoisie* and recognition of the independent Sovereign Status of India as a state are also there.

Unless it were so, there would be no point in making the slogan of "the defence of the national independence and freedom of India" the basic slogan for the coming phase of mass struggles in Inida as was done by Cominform Editorial article. Neither would there be any point in raising the demand that Nehru Government should enter into an alliance with democratic camp led by the Sino-Soviet bloc. How could he enter into such alliance without any semblance of power?

What use would the reformist colonial bourgeoisie of India make of the formal sovereign power granted to them is a seperate matter. We all know that the Indian bourgeoisie would be the last to cut off their subservient imperialist colonial entanglements. But that does not do away with the fact that the Indian bourgeoisie as the new ruling class have the absolute legal and political power in their hands to extricate themselves from those entanglements and enter into whatever international alliances and diplomatic line-up they like by virtue of the independent Sovereign status of India. It should not be forgotten that it is the bourgeois Congress government under Nehru which has kept India interlinked with the British Commonwealth—not British imperialism, or British Parliament.

Split amongst the bourgeoisie on the issue of * power'

Transfer of formal sovereign power and constitutionally unfettered ruling authority into their hands (i.e. the bourgeoisie) formed as a matter of fact the basis of the alliance between Indian bourgeoisie and Anglo-American imperialism. Moreover it should also be noted that this final act of compromise between

142

imperialism and the Congress as the major bourgeois party has not led to any split in the camp of the bourgeoisie. Liberals, illiberals, Gandhians Swarajists, parliamentarians, non-parliamentarians, former 'lefts' and 'Socialists' are all united behind the ruling party — viz: the Congress and its government. Why? The significance of this major fact should not be overlooked—it is because this means that the entire Indian bourgeoisie feel that they i.e., the class for itself, have got command over ruling power to-day. When we speak of the revolutionary section of the anti-imperialist bourgeoisie today in Stalin's sense of the term employed 25 years ago, we must also ask ourselves who are they? What are their organizations? What are their political organizations and platforms? Have the Bengali bankers and industrialists and the stalwarts of Bengal National Chamber of Commerce ranged in revolutionary array with the workers and peasants against Gujrati-Marwari collaborators of imperialism?

Self-contradictions of the bourgeoisie—plea for class collaboration

Self-contradictions undoubtedly there are; and there must be, amongst the various strata and groups of the bourgeoisie : some are in actual governmental power, some are out of it. The middle and petty-bourgeoisie, small manufacturers etc., are often in sharp conflict with the big bourgeoisie. The party of the working class must take advantage of these. But does that mean that the "national" bourgeoisie, or a major section of it, are split from the big bourgeoisie in the same sense in which Stalin spoke in 1925?

It is clear to any Marxist-Leninist beyond any shadow of doubt that self-contradictions in the camp of the bourgeoisie cannot be used as a plea for class-collaboration or alliance with the latter. And it is also clear that here isolated sentences torn from their context from the entirely correct Leninist analysis given by Stalin with reference to conditions obtaining in India

25 years ago, are being sought to be used, now in 1950, as a cover for a "broad nation-wide united front" with the "national bourgeoisie" and open class-collaboration in the expectation that the support of this bourgeoisie might be pressed into service for aligning India with the Sino-Soviet bloc.

It should be noted however that Stalin did not plead even then, in favour of a "broad nation-wide front" in which the "national bourgeoisie" was also to be included. The exact word of Stalin's directive contained in the address to UTE were as follows:

"To set up a *national revolutionary-bloc of workers, peasants and revolutionary intelligentsia* against the bloc of the compromising national bourgeoisie and imperialism."

The "national" bourgeoisie had no place in this revolutionary anti-imperialist bloc of which Stalin spoke in 1925.

This was of course long before the days of "peaceful co-existence of capitalism and Socialism side by side" and "people's Democracy. [2]

India a colonial country still?

The entire theoretical basis of the new stand of the CPI and the Mao version of People's Democracy stands or falls with objective verity of the contention that India is a colonial country still, even after 'transfer of power' to the Indian bourgeoisie, and it is primarily a bourgeois-democratic revolution which historically remains as the order of the day, even now. And, if India is a colonial country even now, then there can be no sense in talking of a Socialist revolution, or basing the strategy and tactics of the working class party on those of a proletarian Socialist revolution for the overthrow of capitalism and the building up of Socialism. There can be no "one-stage" revolution or skipping-over of the democratic stage. This again is elementary Marxism-Leninism. It is from the premise or

144

contention of the backward stage of economic development of a colonial country that Mao Tse Tung's arguments about "the necessity of permitting the existence for a long period of the capitalist economy.......even after the nationwide victory of the revolution" are deduced. The same set of arguments are now being applied to India also, in order to prove that Socialism is nowhere near about the order of the day in the coming phase of mass struggles in India. The entire perspective is that of a democratic revolution or a democratic anti-imperialist national liberation struggle, and of the strategy of broad nationwide united *front* including the "national liberation movement.

The bourgeoisie must be treated as an ally and all talk of Socialism or Socialist revolution must stop because India is a *colonial* country.

India has not been "decolonised"

No Marxist-Leninist would perhaps contend (except the renegade M. N. Roy) that because British imperialism has handed over power to the Indian bourgeoisie, through a backdoor compromisist deal arrived with latter as a mutual safeguard against the rising post-war revolutionary upsurge, India has been decolonised. Lenin had pointed out long ago in his classic analysis of the imperialist phase of capitalism that an essentially colonial status is not entirely incompatible with formal political independence and sovereignty.

Finance capital is such great..., such a decisive force in all economic and international relations, that it is capable of subordinating to itself,and actually does subordinate to itself, even states enjoying complete political independence (Imperialism : P74, Selected Works).

Hence he referred to a variety of forms of dependence, to :

countries which formally are politically independent, but which are, in fact, enmeshed in a net of financial and economic dependence.

Overhaul of the colonial status

The transfer of full political rights and sovereign power to the Indian bourgeoisie means that the order of colonial status has been radically overhauled on the basis of practical political and economic exigencies of the highest stage of finance-capitalism and its inevitable post-war crisis. Threatened by the impact of an almost insuperable economic crisis on the one hand, and by the tidal waves of revolutionary mass upheavals in.the colonies themselves on the other, this overhauling and readjustment of the previously existing political and economic relationship of Britain with India in collusion with the national bourgeoisie, was under the circumstances, the only possible way out for crisis-ridden British imperialism. While considering the significances of this overhauling of the colonial status of India and the transition to a new or higher, or more subtle, disguised form of that status i.e. the status of financial and diplomatic dependence in spite of formal political independence —the satellite status) we must not loose sight of the following two basic facts:

1) That political power has been transferred to the Indian bourgeoisie, and the Indian bourgeoisie represented by the leadership of the Congress was installed in the position of direct ruling authority in place of imperialism vis-a-vis the masses.

2) That India is not a backward colonial country industrially undeveloped, with little or no proletariat or a comparatively small proletariat, say like Indo-China, Morocco or even China; it has rather been always regarded as a capitalistically developed colony with a comparatively large proletariat (and a politically mature and comparatively well-organised national bourgeoisie).

The self-expansion of this bourgeoisie in the period between two world wars and the relative importance of their share in the capital invested in banking, trade and industries in

146

this country— particularly during the second world war-has also to be borne in mind. This has not certainly made them co-equals of the British or American finance-capitalists, or the capitalists of the advanced metropolitan countries, either in economic power or the international ramifications of their vested interests. Neither has their financial or political dependence on British and American capitalists become any less thereby. But the increase in the relative share of the Indian bourgeoisie in the exploitation of the Indian market, their self-expansion i.e., combined with the transfer of political power in their hands and their installation to the position of the new ruling class in place of foreign imperialism, as well as the recognition of the formal sovereign independent status of India, which cannot but involve a corresponding shift in the class alignments and correlationship of forces in India are factors which a Marxist-Leninist could ill afford to ignore.

A truncated half-baked bourgeois revolution

We are confronted with the same historical situation the possibility of which Lenin envisaged in the context of the bourgeois democratic phase of revolution in Russia as early as 1905 :

If the forces of revolutionary working class and peasantry prove inadequate for a decisive victory (of the revolution over Tsarism) the matter will end in a deal between Tsarism and the most 'inconsistent' and most 'self-seeking' elements of the bourgeoisie....Tsarism will have the time to conclude the deal which is already in preparation by Messieurs the Bulygins on the one side and Messieurs the Struves on the other...The whole thing will end in a curtailed constitution, or if the worst comes to the worst, in a travesty of a constitution. This will be an *abortive, half-baked* bourgeois revolution.

Are we not also witnessing a similar process of an *abortive, miscarried, half baked* bourgeois-democratic revolution in India with the bourgeoisie installed in ruling power through a backdoor compromisist deal with imperialism?

Tasks of Bourgeois-Democratic Revolution—not yet completed

The coming to power of the bourgeoisie do not certainly mean that the fundamental tasks of bourgeois-democratic revolution have been completed. But it means that within the generic colonial and dependent status of India—('a capitalistically developed colonial country' —Stalin) there has occurred a transfer of direct ruling power from the hands of one class viz: British finance-capitalism and native feudalism to the hands of another viz: the native Indian bourgeoisie. To *that extent,* and *to that extent only,* the bourgeois-democratic revolution has been completed in **a** "truncated, half-baked, abortive manner" as Lenin envisaged and from a colony under the direct rule of British imperialism and native feudalism India became a semi-colonial, satellite capitalist state dependent on British finance-capital (one of the 'transitional' forms of dependence and subservience to finance-capital and imperialism to which Lenin drew our attention in 'Imperialism') with the national bourgeoisie, and not imperialism-feudalism, as the direct ruling power.

Is India a Colonial country? Historical relevancy of the Russian Analogy

The stock-argument of present day Stalinists against this characterisation of the political and economic status of India is that a historical analogy drawn from the Russian context does not apply to India. Because Russia was an imperialist country whereas India is a colonial country; and the fundamental distinction drawn between the situation in an imperialist country and a colonial country is one of the basic elementary principles of Marxism-Leninism.

This is undeniably true. But at the sametime we must not also forget that Russia was far from the status of the most

148

advanced finance capitalistic and metropolitan imperialist country of the same order as that of Britain, France, Germany or USA. Russia was an 'imperialist' country where queerly enough even the bourgeois-democratic phase of revolution was not completed and feudal autocracy continued to rule till February 1917. The bourgeois democratic revolution in Russia was not as a matter of fact completed till the Socialist phase of revolution began in October 1917. Russia was thus an 'imperialist' country where a feudal aristocracy, instead of the finance-capitalistic bourgeoisie, was the direct ruling class till February 1917. The entire economic life of Russia was under the absolute domination of foreign finance-capitalism (predominantly French & British) till the Socialist revolution of October 1917. Hence Lenin did not characterise Tsarist Russia simply as an 'imperialist' country without any qualification, but rather as a 'militarist-feudal' imperialist country, (cf. Stalin, 'Foundations of Leninism' Pp. 16-17). The socio-historical and political significance of this specific Leninist characterisation of Russian imperialism must in no case be lost sight of. To the extent that Russia remained under the domination of feudal autocracy and foreign finance-capitalism, to the extent that the bourgeois-democratic revolution remained unfulfilled there, to that extent the historical situation in Russia was bound to have certain broad similarities to the situation of colonial and semi-colonial countries like India. For the strategic objective of revolution in these countries and in Tsarist Russia was broadly the same, in first instance viz: the overthrow of the rule of feudalism and foreign finance-capitalism. In countries like India foreign finance-capitalism ruled directly in alliance with a subservient feudal aristrocracy and princedom. In Russia foreign finance-capitalism ruled indirectly behind the facade of the seemingly absolute, militarist-autocratic rule of Tsarism and native feudalism.

Interweaving of 'democratic' and 'Socialist' phases of revolution

We would degenerate into hair-brained dogmatists if we simply go on repeating by rote that Russia was an 'imperialist' country and 'India' remains a 'colonial' country, without taking into account the concrete distinguishing features between an imperialist country and an imperialist country, those between a colony and a colony. As a matter of fact as Lenin pointed out in 1917 that "the division of the world into two principal groups—of colony owning (imperialist) countries on the one hand and colonies on the other—is not the only typical feature of this period, there is also a variety of forms of dependence." Logically this implies that there are a corresponding variety of inter-linking or interweaving (cf. Stalin, ibid pp 17-19) ot tne oourgeois-democratic and Socialist tasks of revolution confronting the proletariat of different countries. Stalin also drew our attention to this cardinal historic fact in 1925 in his address to the UTE with reference to colonial East:

The peculiarity of the colonies and dependent countries at the present time is that a single and all embracing colonial East no longer exists. In earlier days the colonial East was pictured as something single and homogeneous. This picture no longer corresponds to the truth.

India a capitalistically developed colony'

It was on this basis that Stalin drew a fundamental distinction between conditions in China and those in India. And his disciples today, would however seek to quote the self-same Stalin, with glosses from Mao, in order to prove that because India is a colonial country, so India must follow the *China-way;* and because India must follow the China-way, so it will be necessary to stop all talks about Socialist Revolution and to permit the prolonged existence of Capitalism even after the 'nation-wide' victory of democratic revolution. The latest Mao

150

version of Stalinism and Mao Tse-Tung's theory about "the necessity of permitting the existence of capitalism for a long period" on the plea of economic backwardness of colonial countries, not only militates against the earlier Lenin-Stalin theory about concrete historical peculiarities subsisting between imperialist countries each other and those between colonial countries amongst themselves, they equally militate against Lenin's celebrated admonition about the interrelation between the democratic and Socialist phases of revolution in the present day world. "To attempt to raise an aritficial Chinese wall between the democratic and the Socialist revolutions" said Lenin in 1917 — "to seperate them *by anything else than* the degree of preparedness of the proletariat and the degree of its unity with the poor peasants means monstrously, to distort Marxism, to vulgarise it, to substitute liberalism in its place."

The Proletarian Revolution and the Renegade Kautsky

The present day Mao-Stalinists of India precisely resort to this sort of distortion and vulgarisation of Marxism by postulating the "economic backwardness" of colonies as the reason for envisaging a prolonged existence of capitalism after the victory of democratic revolution even in the case of "capitalistically developed" colonies such as India. In former times these would be regarded as nothing but Menshevik deviations pure and simple.

It must however be pointed out here in legitimate defence of Mao, that when he spoke of the necessity of permitting the prolonged existence of capitalism in China (a thoroughly Menshevik conception though,) he had in mind the context of "the backwardness of Chinese economy." He atlcast did not originally confuse between the conditions obtaining in India with those in China in the manner of his Indian followers.

Meaning of the China-Way

The *China-way* of Mao was however foisted on India

151

and on all colonial countries by the Cominform leadership in order to bring round the Indian Party to the course of class-collaboration and appeasement of the "national" bourgeoisie, to the course of seeking "fellow travellers" from capitalist ranks. For a denial of the prespective of a Socialist revolution in the name of democratic national liberationist struggle in the colonies or a colonial national revolution at once opens the way for an alliance (however temporary) with the 'national' bourgeoisie, on which pretext issues of proletarian class-struggle against the capitalists and against capitalism as such may be subsumed under the larger issue of the national-liberation struggle against foreign imperialism. That is the precise historic meaning of the China-way.

Why we must go beyond China-way to a Socialist revolution

It goes without saying of course, that the smashing of the imperialist, finance-capitalist thraldom to which the ruling Indian bourgeoisie have kept the masses of Indian people yoked till now in their own interest, is one of the major historical tasks of coming phase of revolution. Overthrow and liquidation of feudalism is an equally fundamental task which the Indian proletariat will have to undertake in that phase. But as Lenin pointed out repeatedly, the most crucial issue in all revolutions is constituted by the question of power, and which class wields that power at any particular historical moment. For it is only by overthrowing that class that the proletariat could hope to place itself in the position wherefrom to solve the problems of revolution and carry out the historic tasks that confront it. In the specific historical context of India where the bourgeoisie have been installed to the position of a ruling class in collusion with imperialism, the tasks of the democratic revolution will have to be carried out by methods of class struggle, and a class revolution waged against the bourgeoisie, and by overthrowing the ruling bourgeoisie from power. The anti-imperialist and anti-feudal democratic phase of the revolution certainly remain on the historic order of the day. But in order to carry out the task of that phase, we have first to overthrow and dislodge the capitalist class from power. Because it is the power of the capitalist class and bourgeois-dom which acts as the defence barrier or cover for imperialist exploitation. This means, in other words, that to the extent that power is wielded by the Indian capitalist class as the new ruling authority, the historical perspective of an anti-capitalist, Socialist revolution, a revolution for the overthrow of the rule of capital, for totally doing away with all vestiges of imperialist feudal exploitation and carrying forward the democratic revolution to its logical culmination, for establishing the rule of toilers and the dictatorship of the proletariat, and passing over on that basis to the phase of Socialist revolution—also comes to the fore front.

There can be no progress without an advance towards Socialism

Formerly the denial of the perspective of the Socialist revolution in such historical conditions as those in India today, where the bourgeoisie is installed in actual ruling power, on the plea of the democratic phase of revolution, would be condemned even by Stalinists themselves as unalloyed Menshevik deviation from the line of revolutionary Marxism-Leninism. "This current objection (against the perspective of a Socialist Revolution) one that is usually raised in the bourgeois, Socialist-Revolutionary and Menshevik press", Lenin pointed out thirtythree years ago — "is nothing but a reactionary defence of backward capitalism" (cf. India). "We are not ripe for Socialism, it is claimed, it is too early to 'introduce' Socialism, our revolution is a bourgeois revolution, and therefore we must be the menials of the bourgeoisie."

Lenin further added,

The pseudo-Marxist servitors of the bourgeoisie who argue in this way do not understand, what imperialism is, what capitalist monopoly is, what the State is, and what revolutionary democracy is. For if they did understand, they would be bound to admit *that there can be no progress without an advance towards Socialism.*

The only difference between 'pseudo-Marxist servitors of the bourgeoisie' in Lenin's days and their confreres now, lies in the fact that instead of expressing a desire "to become menials of bourgeoisie" they arrogate to themselves the proud position of the "friends and allies" of the bourgeoisie, and seek to treat the bourgeoisie not as "national enemies but allies." That is the basic content of the *China-way* and the Cominform directive to CPI.

Notes:

1. Certain sections of the "big bourgeoisie" do as a matter of fact place themselves in the "broad nation-wide united front" in the Stalinist conception of People's Democracy. This has been clearly pointed out by the American Stalinist writer Frederick. V. Field early last year in course of explaining Mao Tse-Tung's Thesis of New Democracy. "The vital social forces of the new democracy" comments Field after giving a quotation from Mao about multi-class united dictatorship, "are the proletariat, the peasants, the intelligentsia, and other petty bourgeois elements... The coalition will also include important sectors of the middle bourgeoisie and certain sections of the big bourgeoisie". (Pol, affairs, Jan. 1949).

2. For the full text of Stalin's address see: 'On the Colonial question'— Lenin, Stalin, Zhukov.